Seven Tools to Transform Genius into Practical Power

Seven Tools to Transform Genius into Practical Power

Create A Manual To Operate Your Life

Adrian S. Windsor Ph. D

Writer's Showcase
presented by *Writer's Digest*
San Jose New York Lincoln Shanghai

Seven Tools to Transform Genius into Practical Power
Create A Manual To Operate Your Life

Writer's Showcase
presented by *Writer's Digest*
an imprint of iUniverse.com, Inc.

For information address:
iUniverse.com, Inc.
5220 S 16th, Ste. 200
Lincoln, NE 68512
www.iuniverse.com

ISBN: 0-595-12988-9

Printed in the United States of America

Contents

Preface

Life on the front porch

When I was a child growing up in a small Michigan town, I lived on Elm Street. It was a street lined with maple trees, not elm trees. The houses had front porches, and they represented a way of life. In the evening, from early spring through autumn when it got too cold, we would gather on the front porch. Those porches would be equipped in a variety of ways. Our first house at 612 Elm Street had a porch swing, and I spent long summer afternoons reading and swinging on that porch. When we moved to 604 Elm Street, the porch was screened in. That meant that we could enjoy the evening breeze mosquito-free, and even have a lamp for reading because we didn't need to worry about the light attracting insects. Most porches had a glider. A glider is a sofa that sways back and forth, situated firmly on the surface of the porch, not suspended like a swing. Sometimes people had hammocks on their porches, but the problem with a hammock was that it could only accommodate one person.

The front porch represented a way of life. Because it was a front porch, it faced the street and the sidewalk. The houses on both sides of the street thus faced each other. We could look into the windows of our neighbors, and they could look into ours. We always knew who was on the porch and who was in the house, who was home and who wasn't. There was constant movement, house to house and porch to porch. We knew what the neighbors were having for supper, we knew when they were fighting, and we even knew what they were fighting about. We knew that some people preferred to "keep to themselves," and we knew that some people were "nosey." But we really knew that if anyone needed help, all they had to do was yell. When we entered each other's houses, that is across the front porch and into the front door, we would yell, "You hoo! Is anybody home?" Of course, we knew already.

One big chat room.

In today's way of looking at the world, one would say we were networked, organized as one big chat room. We moved outward, block by block, but our own block was our center, and we knew it. We had tolerance for each other's idiosyncrasies and differences; it was forced upon us in order to live together. We learned to speak up when the neighbor's kids did something wrong; and we learned quickly that sooner or later, usually sooner, we would get "told on" if we wandered outside the mark. That mark was clearly defined, not by written words but by neighborhood practice. In other words, the ethical standards and the moral values were firm. No one seemed to think very much about what they had or didn't have. Some of the neighbors got a new car every other year. And some of the neighbors just kept their old cars. Some things the neighbors did were your business, and some things were none of your business. Most of the time we knew the difference. When we got too nosey, we might get told, "It's none of your business."

When life revolved around the front porch, especially in summer, there was a sense of peace and prosperity. The father would come home from work, have supper, maybe work in the yard, and then go sit on the front porch. Some mothers worked, too; but as soon as the chores were done, they would come out on the porch. The Armstrongs, who were Catholic and had lots of kids, worked as a team from home. They "hung wallpaper." It would not be the right thing to do to ask anyone but the Armstrongs to hang your wallpaper; they had so many kids and they worked so hard. The Hansons had a beer tavern, so Mr. Hanson worked late. It was ok for the Hansons to be in the beer business, because they were German and Germans drink beer. Actually, the whole neighborhood was called German Hill because so many of the neighbors were German.

The front porch tolerance

As kids, we played in the street and moved back and forth to each other's porches. At 6:15 we would gather on the steps of one of our porches to watch the nuns walk from Sienna Heights College to St. Joseph's Church. It was a mystery what they had under their black and white habits. My father said they shaved their heads. When we were told to come in, that meant to come home to our own porch. We might still be carrying on a conversation with the kids next door, just porch to porch instead of hip to haunch. Sometimes we played kick the can, sometimes hide and seek, sometimes tag, sometimes school, and sometimes doctor. We were all better at some things than at others, and we accepted deficiency as a given. Harold C., for instance, "wasn't all there," so he could play hide and seek, but he couldn't play school. It wasn't a good idea to play doctor with Walter A. in the bushes because he conducted physical examination in such detail.

I remember when my cousin, Wanda, moved out of town, and I went there to baby sit. The houses were all in a row, but none had a front porch. Instead, there was a garage door facing the street. All of the houses looked exactly alike. Her children were supposed to play only in the back yard, and they weren't allowed on the street. In the evening what they really liked to do was just watch television. It made it easy to baby sit. They had a concrete patio in the back, but it wasn't screened in, and they didn't go out there too often. Their back yard was separated from the neighbors on both sides by a fence, and each family kept to itself. Wanda liked it better that way because she didn't have the neighbors bothering her. She was too busy for that. She was a nurse.

Our houses and our porches metaphorically express our orientation not only to our world, but also to our experiences. R. Buckminster Fuller, the inventor of the geodesic dome, cared about houses. Much of his life work was spent trying to figure out how to house all of humanity. Since the tools I offer here evolved from concepts explored in his *Operating Manual for Spaceship Earth*, there is an underlying assumption that the planet is our house, fully exposed and fully networked within Universe. Life lived from the garage door symbolizes the rat race, separation and anxiety: "making ends meet." Life lived from the front porch is more tranquil, peaceful, harmonious, under beneficent control. I believe we can live again from the front porch.

This spaceship we're riding on is really quite small, and we can't avoid acknowledging we inhabitant the same house. The Internet shrinks its size a little more every day. It is important that we mind each other's business, that we be our brother's keepers, that we know the rules, that we take advantage of shared resources, that we be tolerant of each other's differences, that we each develop our true wealth, and that we use every tool available to do it. This book, *Seven Tools to*

Transform Genius into Practical Power, has as its subtitle, *Create a Manual to Operate Your Life.* These tools are meant to take you out of the rat race, into control; out of the garage, into the leisure and peace of the front porch.

Acknowledgements

In writing this book, the many hundreds of students who have passed through my classroom have been my greatest teachers. For a lifetime of spiritual and intellectual nourishment, I thank those teachers who have inspired and encouraged me. At the University of Michigan, these teachers fed the hungry and impressionable Sharon Wood from Adrian, Michigan: Prof. Austin Warren who first introduced me to Emerson, Dickinson, Hawthorne and the metaphysical poets; Professor Bennett Weaver for his moving interpretations of Browning, Dante, the Romantic Poets, and the Bible; Professor Gerald Else for his heroic presentation of the classics; Professor William Frankena for his voyages to Plato's realm of Ideas; Professor G. B. Harrison for his explication and vigorous reading of Shakespeare; Professor James Gindin for his introduction to modern British fiction, especially Woolf and Lawrence; and Professor Herbert Barrows for piloting me through theses on first James Joyce and then Virginia Woolf. I thank also those later teachers of my spiritual development, in particular Dr. Peggy Bassett and my dear friend and mentor, Joyce Gardner. Dr. Jackie Belzano, classmates, and workshop participants in my San Juan Capistrano community contributed to my clarity and purpose. Two great musicians gave me special encouragement: Norm Douglas served as my creative booster when I made the commitment to set other activities aside and to get the book written, and Suz Ogden bought the first book a year before it came into print. I kept her $20 bill in a conspicuous place to remind me to deliver the end product. My dear friend, Patty Truman, offered compassionate understanding, prayerful support, a discriminating reading of the manuscript, and gentle guidance. My daughter, Kerren Bergman, read my manuscript with fastidious detail, formatted the exercises, gave computer instruction, offered painstaking criticism and total loving support. I can't thank her enough. My son, Charles Proudfit, brought to bear the clear, white light of intellectual challenge, the pragmatic estimation of a man of business, and a sensitive and nourishing spiritual center and focus. Although I did not always take his advice, I accepted his guidance and the text is vastly improved because of it. My parents, LeRoy and Delores Wood, and my grandparents, Cecelia and Columbach Happel and Flora May Wood, are the soil from which all growth of this tiny seed has occurred. To Ronald Knapp, my partner in life, I offer thanks for his humor, his constant encouragement and support, his patience when I spent long hours at the computer, his exercise of the bragging rights that I long ago relinquished to him, and his brilliant suggestion that we create and copyright a graphic design derived from the Mountain of Light as a corporate logo, thus making it available for the cover of this book.

Beware when the great God lets loose a thinker on this planet. Then all things are at risk. It is as when a conflagration has broken out in a great city, and no man knows what is safe, or where it will end. There is not a piece of science but its flank may be turned to-morrow; there is not any literary reputation, not the so-called eternal names of fame, that may not be revised and condemned. The very hopes of man, the thoughts of his heart, the religion of nations, the manners and morals of mankind are all at the mercy of a new generalization. Generalization is always a new influx of the divinity into the mind. Hence the thrill that attends it.

Emerson, Circles [1]

Introduction

Housing for humanity

In the early eighties I was led to make a public commitment to bring the ideas of R. Buckminster Fuller to the public. Although Fuller is best known as the inventor of the geodesic dome, as one reviews his lifetime of invention, it is apparent that the dome was the last of many designs he created out of his compassionate concern for housing humanity. He wanted to produce portable houses that could be dropped into the most remote deserts, the deepest forests, and the highest mountains. His intention was to use these houses domestically, but in fact the military probably took the greatest advantage of his designs.

Our human preference for living in rectangular boxes kept his inventions other than the dome from ever taking off and gaining wide acceptance. Furthermore, his skills as a business man were not as developed as his inventive genius. The house that he designed in Wichita, Kansas at the end of World War II to take advantage of aircraft materials never came on the market. He had hundreds of orders, but refused to begin production until he had made just one more prototype. His financial partners insisted that he relinquish control over production, he refused, and the company went under, one of several bankruptcies.

The geodesic dome

The geodesic dome is definitely Fuller's most important invention. In fact, he is known so much for this invention that when, in 1996, three chemists, Harold Kroto of England's University of Sussex, and Richard Smalley and Robert Curl of Rice University in Houston, were awarded the Nobel Peace Prize for the discovery of a molecule shaped like a geodesic dome, they named it after him. They called the molecules, formed in the crystal residue that results from mixing helium with the carbon vapor produced by zapping graphite with a laser beam, "buckminsterfullerenes," shortened to "buckyballs." These molecules, composed of 60 carbon atoms, have hollow interiors that make them extremely valuable for conduction of electricity and drug delivery systems.

The fascination with the geodesic dome took Fuller to college campuses and to speaking engagements all over the world. There he shared his demonstration of the integrity of geometric shapes and his passionate commitment to the future of humanity, often in lectures that would extend from three hours to sometimes days. He delivered his lectures in long and convoluted sentences using vocabulary that could leave the audience baffled. His enthusiasm, however, made one feel, at least for that moment, enlightened and inspired. In retrospect, it may have been pretentious, but the zeal dispelled the critical predilection of the audience. His writing is written as he speaks, and most of his books have a co-writer who attempted to re-phrase and re-structure in order to make the presentation of his ideas more comprehensible.

The commitment

My commitment to promote Fuller's teach
during a seminar with the stated purpose of empowering people to be more effective in their lives. Fuller's ideas were at the
core of this seminar, especially the concepts of leverage and
synergy. Both words now have such common occurrence in
our everyday speech that it seems amazing that groups of
knowledgeable and essentially well-educated people would
come together to be introduced to these ideas as fresh and
vital. Yet here I am writing about them again in a way that I
think will be meaningful to you. Certainly, since speaking
intent attracts the flow of events and resources to make ideas
reality, I must regard it as a natural evolution from Fuller's
inspiration that this book has taken form.

I am a business woman, a real estate broker and the head of
a privately held corporation, yet by education and professional
training, I am also an educator. Although I left formal *academia* almost two decades ago, I am still teaching and will probably always be teaching in whatever I do. At the heart of the
experience is the relationship between teacher and student,
that cottage industry where it all began, with the itinerant
teacher sharing the word with anyone who would listen, from
Socrates onward. In formal *academia*, as frequently happens
with good teachers, I found myself "elevated" to administration, not realizing that in entering bureaucracy, I was aban-
doning my essential nature, that of the entrepreneur.

Always sales

The teacher in the classroom is an entrepreneur, taking her
product to market, so to speak, and convincing the buyer that

life without it will not really be worth living. I tell my students today that "Life is sales!" Selling Homer, Sophocles and Aeschyulus to undergraduates at 8:00 a.m., in retrospect, was actually a bigger and more momentous challenge than selling a million dollar house or a forty million dollar office building. It was only after leaving *academia*, entering business, and then re-entering the classroom, that I thoroughly understood my role in that position of leadership, not as one who keeps and dispenses information and gives grades to punish and reward, but rather as one who offers an opportunity for transformation. It seemed appropriate, as my business makes it increasingly difficult to set time aside for classroom teaching, that I now put my teaching into book form, actually "practicing what I preach": leverage.

World Game

In the mid-eighties, I had begun to strengthen my understanding of Fuller's ideas by participating in a reading group in Boulder, Colorado where we endeavored to comprehend the ideas presented in his convoluted syntax. I also began to fulfill my commitment to share Fuller's ideas by bringing an experiential version of his "world game" to the community during a World Affairs Conference held at the University. A dymaxion rendering of the planet was spread out on the gymnasium floor, reflecting the configuration of the continents before the shift that pulled them apart. People stood in each country in proportion to the population, both the United States and Canada, sparsely populated, India so crowded it was almost impossible to find enough room for the required number. As one plays this game, the disparity between the distribution of population and resources on the planet becomes very clear: food, energy, water, raw materials. For instance, loaves of bread symbolized the amount of food consumed. The people in the United States were loaded down with loaves of bread. All of India had only one. One-fourth of the world's population is now in India.

Fuller and Emerson

It was, however, not until 1991, after I moved to California, that I got "down to brass tacks." The Dean at Coastline Community College, a campus without walls that serves more adults and immigrants than traditional-aged students, invited me to come and teach a writing course. At that time I had been away from teaching for almost a decade, and I agreed to accept on the condition that I be able to select the texts that would generate the subject matter of the students' writing. My choice was Fuller's *Operating Manual for Spaceship Earth* and Emerson's *Essays*, moving from the planet to the inner self, a voyage that I still create each semester. This is my community service, a calling, in the sense that Emerson speaks of "vocation."

My students leave the class as good writers, and many also go through life transformations. My purpose as a teacher is to provide tools to make them more effective in whatever they undertake in life. Some of these tools are drawn from the concepts that underlie Fuller's *Operating Manual for Spaceship Earth*,[2] the manual, he contends, that we have created and developed over the history of mankind through our discovery of how our planet operates, through the evolution of our "know how." With Emerson's inspiration, we discover that each of us has an unique ability, a special calling, an "inner genius," waiting to be acknowledged and tapped. The class challenges the students to use Fuller's concepts as tools to express and to empower that "inner genius." Emerson expresses my function as a teacher in the concluding words of his essay, "Experience": "The transformation of genius into practical power." [3]

The transforming process

This transforming process takes a while; and frequently as a teacher I am discouraged, until suddenly, it's as if the students, one by one, cross over a threshold, reach the plateau and begin to soar. For example, one of my former students stopped by my class one evening when he had another class in the same building. He is a Marine reservist whose trained military profession is purchasing. He is completing his AA degree, has been accepted at Pepperdine University to pursue his bachelor's degree, and has started his own business. He attributes the success of his entrepreneurial "start-up" to thinking like a "great pirate" and employing the concept of leverage he learned in my class. He said, "Well how's it going?" I said, "We're in process. They don't quite get it yet." He said, "They will. It all comes together at the end."

Derivation and integration

When *Operating Manual for Spaceship Earth* went out of print in 1995, I continued to teach seven concepts derived from Fuller's book as tools for abundant "livingry." Although *Operating Manual for Spaceship Earth* is one of Fuller's most readable books, his style, replicating his manner of speech, left most students baffled, especially when he speaks of his general systems theory. It has worked best for me to draw from his ideas, to translate them into a form readily comprehended by my students, and to assimilate them into my personal expression, drawing as well upon my study of literature and the experience of my lifetime.

It would be inappropriate for me to assert that in reading this book, you will get the fundamental ideas of R. Buckminster Fuller. For that you must go to the man and his actual works. Rather, what I offer here is purely derivative, a down-to-earth, meat and potatoes, simplified application of some of his ideas, the result of classes and workshops where specific tools have evolved to equip my students to re-examine where they are and to empower them to move to wherever they wish to go, their "big picture." My audience is the unsophisticated reader who wishes to make basic changes in his life and to establish a workable plan for manifesting his dreams.

Perfect Universe: Perfect Intelligence

The thesis of *Operating Manual for Spaceship Earth* is that the planet came without an operating manual so that human beings who reside here can figure out the way it works. It works perfectly, indeed, has always worked perfectly. The only thing that changes is our understanding. Here at the beginning of the twenty-first century, our knowledge is growing exponentially, and revisions in our understanding are coming so quickly we can hardly absorb them. Fuller assumes a perfect intelligence created this perfectly operating planet, and he presents the concepts and principles that inform that operation. He calls this "livingry" and ardently challenges us to use these concepts and principles to get our share of the natural abundance, so obviously provided by this perfect intelligence whom he calls "Universe" and I call God. I invite you now to share in these *Seven Tools for the Transformation of Genius into Practical Power*. The exercises at the ends of the chapters are designed to empower you, the reader, should you elect to do so, to create a manual to operate your life.

Past ideas and present belief

Climate of opinion

We all bring to wherever we are whatever we have come to *believe* based on our personal experience. I picked up ideas on the front porch that have been with me most of my life, some useful, some destructive, some limiting. Since effective change can only take place when we know how we got to *believe* what we *believe*, we will begin with an examination of the belief system that many of us carry around, created by a combination of climate of opinion and race consciousness. When I use the term "climate of opinion," I am referring to the ideas that are integrated into our thinking because of: things our parents have told us; things our teachers, relatives, and friends say or do; things we read in mass publications such as newspapers and the grocery story check-out line magazines; and things the media chooses to stress on television and the radio. Other people's "importances" affect our world view and skew our vision.

Race consciousness

When I use the term "race consciousness," I am adopting but re-phrasing the terminology of Ernest Holmes who wrote of "race suggestion."[5] This was his catch-all term for what we inherit in our belief system from the beginning of man, our prejudices, our attitudes, our fears. It is an envelope of life with origins so deep in our psyche, our "collective unconscious," as defined by Karl Jung, that it often emerges with clarity only in our dreams because it can be so frightening. It may go back to our cave man origins when wind or lightening or thunder threatened our existence. It may have been expressed in philosophy, in religion, in poetry, and so penetrated our thinking that it would never occur to us to think otherwise.

Level playing field

As I examine climate of opinion and race consciousness, my intent is not to pass judgment, but to be aware. As we know and accept the belief systems that have formed, nurtured, and sustained us, they lose their power. This is what the art critic Roger Fry called the "aesthetic experience," the moment when the artist looks at nature and sees it whole so that each of the elements loses its individual importance, and he then is able to paint the canvas as God has painted it, in its entirety. As we release the beliefs or attitudes that control us, hold us back or direct us to self-sabotage, we are more free to take advantage of the tools that Universe has provided for us so plentifully, to give metaphysical application to the physical concepts that make things run, to accept cause and effect and to harness that action and reaction positively in our life.

My trash can

Since I cannot speak for you, I will speak for myself. During those long summer days and evenings on the front porch, I collected and stashed away the climate of opinion and race consciousness that I affectionately call my "trash can." My intent is not so much to beat myself up in public, as it is to just let you know that I've carried around my fair share of garbage, have dumped some, and am working at dumping the rest. You may have some of mine, and I'm sure you have some of your own.

A sample list of these beliefs and attitudes
My trash can picked up on the porch:

* We are living a life sentence.
* Life is a struggle to make ends meet.
* Man is inherently sinful and evil.
* We all have our limits.
* Anything easy isn't worth doing.
* An open path is out of control.
* We are not whole unless we have a mate.
* God keeps score.
* Success and failure are pure luck.

My touchstones

Once we've taken out the trash, we'll be ready to examine the creation of a perfect mind in action, the work of Universe, the masterpiece of a freely giving God. The message is grounded in optimism, confirming the enormous capacity of the human mind and spirit to solve every problem. I am totally in awe of the giving nature of God that manifests as God expressing through man. Throughout this book I have drawn upon my personal touchstones from fiction and poetry, and I have freely used the experiences of my students and myself as illustration and demonstration. We teach what we need to learn. In teaching my students, I have been confirming my faith that there is a perfect pattern for our experience;

that human beings, though frail, susceptible, selfish, and greedy, have an enormous resilience and intuitive impulse toward good; that we can re-invent ourselves and our life in accordance with our chosen vision; that Universe, God, has provided all the tools we need and is just waiting for us to wake up and pay attention.

Seven concepts: seven tools

We will deal with seven concepts derived and distilled from Fuller: Great Pirates, Piano Tops, No Mistakes: Only Opportunities to Discover the Truth, Leverage, Synergy, Big Picture, and True Wealth. Each concept is accompanied by exercises that, of course, are optional. You are invited to participate at your chosen level in self-assessment and analysis, in envisioning your perfect life, in determining the steps you will take, and in integrating the tools provided by Universe into your personal arsenal.

If you choose to follow the complete path, to actually create a manual for your life, you will:

* Become a Great Pirate and take sovereignty over your life.
* Let go of outmoded behavior patterns, Piano Tops.
* Discard irrelevancies, Mistakes, and greet challenges proactively.
* Use Leverage to do more with less.
* Create Synergy in your families, your relationships, your work.

* Envision your Big Picture and take command of your navigational path.
* Tap into your True Wealth and accept abundance.

YOU WILL TRANSFORM YOUR GENIUS INTO PRACTICAL POWER!

I'm Nobody! Who are you?
Are you–Nobody—too?
Then there's a pair of us!
Don't tell! They'd banish us—you know!

How dreary—to be—somebody!
How pubic—like a Frog—
To tell your name—the livelong June—
To an admiring Bog.
Emily Dickinson, 1861

From *Sailing to Byzantium*
An Aged man is but a paltry thing,
A tattered coat upon a stick, unless
Soul clap its hands and sing,
and louder sing
For every tatter in its mortal dress.
W. B. Yeats, 1926

From *The Road Not Taken*
I shall be telling this with a sigh
Somewhere ages and ages hence:
Two roads diverged in a wood, and I—
I took the one less traveled by,
And that has made all the difference.
Robert Frost, 1916

Part 1: Life's Sentence

* We all accepted a life sentence, derived from our parents, race consciousness and climate of opinion.

* We aren't stuck with the sentence.

* As masters of our thoughts and directors of our actions, we can choose the *who, what, when, where* and *how* of our life.

No man can learn what he has not preparation for learning, however near to his eyes is the object....God screens us evermore from premature ideas. Our eyes are holden that we cannot see things that stare us in the face, until the hour arrives when the mind is ripened; then we behold them, and the time when we saw them not is like a dream.

Emerson, *Spiritual Laws* [1]

The Sentence

The cat in the bag

I often use the "cat in a bag" analogy to describe my students' sentences. Once an idea is articulated by symbols, once the words are on paper, a commitment is made. No matter how empty of content, no matter how confused the presentation of the ideas, no matter how limited the vocabulary, no matter how poorly constructed the syntax, the sentence exists; and they are determined to deal with it in its present form. They may punch, pull, jab, squeeze, attack, wrench, wiggle, and squiggle, but the basic sentence is still there. They are like a cat caught in a burlap sack, trying to escape, unable to get out, trapped by the context. They are stuck with the sentence, or so it seems. The only solution, the best solution, is to throw the sentence out and start over; but because the sentence *is*, they continue to wrestle with it. The more they struggle, the more their claws are immobilized. I remind them again and again, "It's your sentence. You wrote it; you can get rid of it; you can start over. It's only a sentence." Yet the desire to deal with and fix the status quo, no matter how rotten it is, prevails. They truly believe they are stuck with the sentence.

The judgment

Kafka's short story, "The Judgment,"[2] is about a father, a son, and a sentence. Kafka's works, like the works of all great

3

writers, are about his own unresolved issues, the insecure young man, dissatisfied with his accomplishments because nothing he does is quite good enough, trapped by circumstances and dominated by the powerful, overbearing, unsympathetic and judgmental father. In "The Judgment," the mother has been dead for two years, and the father and son, Georg, are sharing the same house and working together in the business. Since the mother's death, Georg has begun to succeed in the business, and he has even become engaged to be married.

Georg's self-perceived success

The story takes place on a Sunday morning. Georg is writing a letter to a friend who is living in St. Petersburg, Russia, "wearing himself out to no purpose in a foreign country." Georg is reluctant to arouse the friend's envy with the good news of his engagement and his general success since his mother's death: "...perhaps it was mostly due to an accidental run of good fortune—which was very probable indeed—but at any rate during those two years the business had developed in a most unexpected way, the staff had had to be doubled, the turnover was five times as great, no doubt about it, further progress lay just ahead." He shrinks from telling his friend of this success and instead concentrates on local gossip.

The father's perception and definition

When he is finished with his letter, he enters the father's part of the house where he finds him sitting in darkness. As Georg looks at him, he thinks, "My father is still a giant of a man." Quite the contrary, Kafka tells us the father is old, ill, weak, and physically powerless. We begin to sense a discrepancy between Georg's perception and reality. Georg tells the father he has written the letter to the friend. As the conversation between them progresses, as they begin to disagree, we come to understand that the son is a split personality, torn apart between his preferred self-perception and the father's definition of Georg as powerless, inept, and impotent. The father's definition wins out. He defiantly tells Georg the friend in Russia is his friend, not the son's. He denounces Georg's fiancée as a slut who "lifted her skirts." He disparages and discredits Georg as a business man. Georg accepts his abuse, stuffs it.

Covered up

Georg lifts his father into bed, noticing how weak he is, how dirty his underwear is, making a "firm decision to take him into his own future establishment," but observing "the care he meant to lavish there on his father might come too late." This is one of Georg's most honest thoughts, that his father might be dead at last. He can only think it covertly. As Georg attempts to cover his father, the father throws off the blankets exclaiming: "You wanted to cover me up, I know, my young sprig, but I'm far from being covered up yet. And even if this is the last strength I have, it's enough for you, too much for you." When the father stands unsupported and kicks his legs out, demonstrating his power, "Georg shrank into a corner, as far away from his father as possible."

Georg's identity seized

The tension between the two men grows as the father claims Georg has been "strutting through the world, finishing off deals" the father made for him. The father declares, "I am still much the stronger of us two…I've established a fine connection with your friend and I have your customers here in my pocket....Just take your bride on your arm and try getting in my way! I'll sweep her from your very side, you don't know how!" The father lays claim to Georg's whole identity, grabs it away from him.

The sentence: death by drowning

Georg cries out, "So you've been lying in wait for me!" The father replies: "How long a time you've taken to grow up....So now you know what else there was in the world besides yourself, till now you've known only about yourself! An innocent child, yes, that you were, truly, but still more truly have you been a devilish human being!—And therefore take note: I sentence you now to death by drowning."

Georg opens the door, rushes down the stairs and across the street to the bridge: "He swung himself over, like the distinguished gymnast he had once been in his youth to his parents' pride." He lets himself drop in the water, speaking his final lie, his final self-deception, "Dear parents, I have always loved you, all the same."

A gigantic insect

In another of Kafka's works, "The Metamorphosis," the hero, a traveling salesman, hates his job, his employer, and his life. Burdened by the chore of supporting his parents and sister, he awakens one morning and discovers he's a bug: "As Gregor Samsa awoke one morning from uneasy dreams he found himself transformed in his bed into a gigantic insect." As the story unfolds, we see that this is his sentence, imposed upon him by the way he sees himself: Enslaved to his company; enslaved to his parents and the debt they incurred;

accused by his employer of laziness, neglect, possible theft; surrounded by scoundrels and at the mercy of circumstances. By becoming a bug, a giant cockroach, no less, he is escaping from his sentence in life. As a bug he no longer has to go to work, no longer has to do his parents' bidding, no longer has to bow and scrape, to be a machine for other people.

The dung beetle trashed

The family decides that they must "get rid of the old dung beetle." Even his sister, who has treated him with the most kindness, announces he must go: "I won't utter my brother's name in the presence of this creature, and so all I say is we must try to get rid of it." Gregor, who had "not the slightest intention of frightening anyone far less his sister," retreats and his sister slams, bolts, and locks the door behind him, startling him so much that "his little legs gave beneath him." As Gregor breathes his last breath, "He thought of his family with tenderness and love. The decision that he must disappear was one that he held to even more strongly than his sister, if that were possible." The charwoman finds him the next day: "Indeed, Gregor's body was completely flat and dry, as could only now be seen when it was no longer supported by legs and nothing prevented one from looking closely at it." The father, mother, and sister decide to sell the house, to move into a smaller place, to begin a new life. Gregor is gone and forgotten.

Sentenced

Both Georg and Gregor commit suicide. The psychologist, Theodore Reik, observed through his work with clients that depression is rage against someone else turned against yourself; and suicide, likewise, is a death wish against someone near and dear, again turned against yourself. Georg is sentenced by his father, and Gregor sentences himself. In both instances, however, the sentence can only stick if the individual accepts it, owns it, acts upon it. Kafka is extreme, so if you haven't drowned or turned into a bug, take a big, deep, fresh breath. You are, however, sentenced. Someone sentenced all of us. It may be a parent, a spouse, or we ourselves.

But not stuck

We, however, are not stuck with the sentence, for we have the option of writing our own. We are at choice. We may handle our life experience like Georg, acting out someone else's orders, someone else's ideas. We may handle it like Gregor, turning ourselves into a cockroach, escaping from reality by living out a nightmare. Or we may choose to rid ourselves of the sentence and start over. The truth is we need act out the sentence only if we accept it. *We* give the sentence its power. Indeed, the very people who sentenced us usually didn't know they were doing it. They were only living out *their own* sentences.

Our baggage, our stuff

Whenever we begin to think about change, it is helpful to take an inventory of our life sentence. Is it based on what we perceive to be given to us? Did we write our own? Or did we write our own based on what we heard from someone or somewhere else? Whatever we perceive to be our sentence, is our sentence. For what we perceive, what we accept, we take on as our burden. Then we write it out in our own words. It is now ours to be lived out. That's why we call it baggage or our stuff. This is our baggage; this is our block; this is our sentence. I did say, however, that we are at choice. We may choose the guillotine, or we may choose to discard the burden and be free. We may not be able to dump all the baggage in one fell swoop; but if we know it for what it is, we may be able to set it aside for a time, if only to trip over it later on.

The baggage inventory

In my experience, just the ability to identify and to label an emotion, a fear, or a belief, takes away its power. Since I have done this for myself, although I would never claim to be totally baggage-free, I am going to inventory my baggage for you in the next few chapters because I am intimately acquainted with it. It came to me from many sources: my family, the climate of opinion, race consciousness. I picked up some of it on the front porch. From these sources I wrote my own sentence.

The teachings of Fuller and Emerson have encouraged me to let the cat out of the bag, to start over, to rewrite. The following summary of my sentence may or may not resonate with you. You may not have all of my baggage. Good! Chances are, however, you have some of it. And you will have your own, regardless. Let me say this **was** my sentence. I use the past tense, because I hopefully have taught and written it out of myself—not a pretty journey, but a necessary one. Note that my sentence is plural. It always takes more than one: one to speak and one to hear.

My Sentence
We must make ends meet because we are inherently evil.

I grew up believing that in life, we have to make ends meet. This can only be done through struggle because we were meant to struggle. Since there actually isn't quite enough for everybody, we have to get ours. God set us up for it from the very beginning. The minute the serpent tempted Eve and together they tempted Adam to eat that apple, we were doomed. No matter how pure we may appear on the outside, inside we are evil. For those who call this sin, there's a way out with a savior. If we don't like to label this predicament as sin, and have not accepted a savior, then at the best we must see man as a social animal, creating and perpetually tangled in social problems needing resolution. Either way, we are inherently corrupt: just flat bad. If that weren't bad enough, we have limits. It really doesn't matter who imposed those limits, because we have to deal with them ourselves.

If it's easy, it's worthless.

Because there isn't enough, because we have to struggle to make ends meet, and because we have our limits, anything that comes too easily has no value. We can only define ourselves through hard work. We may have great potential, halfway up Jacob's ladder, somewhere between the highest of heaven and the lowest of earth, but we have our place. If we rock the boat, we might land in the water and drown. It doesn't matter whether we're right or not. Isn't that the source of the term "dead right?" Who are we to presume and assume that we can slide easily into first base when life was meant from the start to be an immense cat's cradle with us entangled right in the middle?

Emotional ideas rule.

These are the emotional ideas that have ruled my life. It has taken me a lifetime to realize that although my limits were set by my parents, I'm the one who gave them reality, who gave them power. I sentenced myself. As we examine these beliefs in the following chapters, one by one, some may be familiar to you. My intent is that they will fade into the woodwork under the scrutiny of the pure, bright, intellectual light, or at least, like Gregor, hide in the woodwork until they die and decay. It is possible to reverse a life sentence; it is possible to remold and remake the sentence we write for ourselves.

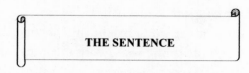

THE SENTENCE

I never thought of myself as being "sentenced." Yet, as I review the attitudes and beliefs I have had about myself, I observe my parents and family had specific expectations about my future. Here are some of the things they said and did that influenced me.

My mother:

_____

_____

_____

_____

_____

My father:

_____

_____

_____

_____

_____

My siblings:

_____

_____

_____

_____

_____

_____

My grandparents:

_____

_____

_____

_____

_____

In school, my earliest memories of my classmates' attitudes toward me are:

_____

_____

_____

_____

As I progressed through school, I reinforced my "public image" by this behavior:

_____

_____

_____

_____

Some of my early childhood behavior patterns that still affect how I deal with challenges are:

We are afraid of truth, afraid of fortune, afraid of death, and afraid of each other. Our age yields no great and perfect persons. We want men and women who shall renovate life and our social state, but we see that most natures are insolvent, cannot satisfy their own wants, have an ambition out of all proportion to their practical force and do lean and beg day and night continually.

Emerson, Self Reliance [1]

Making Ends Meet

Thrift

In Shakespeare's *Hamlet*, when his mother, Gertrude, marries his uncle immediately after his father's mysterious death, "most wicked speed, to post, /With such dexterity to incestuous sheets," Hamlet comments quixotically to Horatio: "Thrift, thrift, Horatio! The funeral baked meats/Did coldly furnish forth the marriage tables." I,ii, 179-81. If you approve of this thrifty idea, using leftovers from the funeral for the wedding banquet the next day, then you probably also add extra water to the soup to stretch it, pour milk in the pan drippings to make gravy, and make one little can of tuna fish feed four people by adding celery and boiled eggs. These are all ways of making ends meet. Thrift is an old Yankee virtue. At issue is when an act ceases to be *thrifty* and is, instead, an expression of a fear that there just is not enough.

Scarcity Consciousness

"Making ends meet," an old saying, comes from fear and anxiety. R. Buckminster Fuller called it the Malthus/Marx/Darwin/Entropy consciousness.[2] This consciousness tells us the planet is running out of food for the people because there are so many of us, that the unenlightened task-masters who do the manual labor are more important than the thinkers, that only the fittest can survive in the "dog eat dog" world we live

16

in, and that in the long run it won't matter anyway because the planet is running out of energy. This is a "doers are more important than thinkers" philosophy.

The Wired, the Kluge, and the Provincial

In an article, "The Fate of a Nation,"[3] published in the "Opinion" section of the *LA Times*, David Friedman divided our populace in the United States into three economies: the Wired, the Kluge (name taken from Rube Goldberg), and the Provincial. His categories, admittedly, are gross generalities, yet they provide a workable framework for understanding this scarcity consciousness and the prevailing climate of opinion. His thesis is that the Wired, the Bill Gates's of the world, should prevail and will determine the fate of the nation because they will hire more people and because the Wired hold the future.

What he observes, however, is that politics is controlled by the Kluge, comprised of: 1) the media and 2) the bureaucrats in public institutions and education. The Wired are too preoccupied in their creative and productive activity to be mired down in the slow pace of bureaucracy. The Provincial dominate in rural America, among blue-collar workers, in conservative political circles; and they are distrustful of the Wired, wary of technology, and challenged by change. We know the Provincial as much for what they're *against* as for what they're *for*. They are against international trade, against NAFTA, against planetary initiatives, against free choice, against welfare, against affirmative action, against U.S. involvement in NATO's military actions and, indeed, any military action where our national interest is not at stake.

Kluge fires and Provincial fears

The scarcity consciousness in the climate of opinion is acted upon, expressed and articulated by the Kluge and the Provincial. The Kluge in politics and *academia* protect the *status quo*, and the Kluge in media exploit the sensational. The power of the Kluge creates a poll-driven President, manipulated by the climate of opinion rather than by principle. The Kluge fuel the predictions of the Provincial that the fabric of our society has come unraveled and that our worst fears are being realized.

The Provincials lament our jobs are being lost to nations with cheap labor, our imbalance of trade is undermining our economy, and our nation is torn apart by sex, immorality, and violence. The message that sells to them is based on fear and scarcity. We must protect what we have. We must circle up the tents to protect the American family, and we must protect our borders because there's scarcely enough for everyone, because it's a struggle in this world to "make ends meet." This thought rules many of our lives; we have given our sovereignty to it.

Up and dressed

When I was a child in Michigan, it was a major accomplishment in the morning to be up and dressed. Even though both of my parents worked, there was usually someone at home with me in the morning, a grandmother, an aunt, a baby sitter. Dressing was leisurely. Before I left for school, Happy Hank would check through the radio with his magic eye to see that the house was left neat and tidy. And then off I would go, a block and a half to school. When it rained I carried a half-broken umbrella, retrieved from a neighbor's trash on pick-up day. The children in my kindergarten class were critical of the umbrella until I told them it was a special umbrella because it was Chinese.

Now, half a century later, contrary to news of the booming economy, I sometimes think the Malthus/Marx/Darwin/Entropy consciousness has proven its validity. As I sit down to write this morning, there are homes all over the United States where one or two parents are arising at 4:00 a.m. to begin their day. This is what they have ahead of them: getting themselves up and dressed; getting the children up and dressed and driven to day care; making the commute to work where they will stay eight or ten or twelve hours; picking their children up from day care.

No relief in sight

The *LA Times* reports the parental strain in an article, "The Six O'Clock Scramble"[4] relating the difficulty for parents, faced with long work days, to get back to day care by 6:00 p.m., the closing time, to pick up their children. The quality of life in America, with all of our mechanical domestic appliances, has not increased along with the gross national product. Again, the *LA Times* carries a headline: "Our Culture of Efficiency Has Made Life Harder."[5] The author, Mary McNamara, observes that "ability to multi-task a must' is now a standard job description tagline, and seminars and workshops continue to appear like toadstools after too much rain." The multi-task tagline is generally directed toward women. The more gadgets and appliances we have to help us, to make our life "easier," the more women are expected to do.

The haves and the have-nots

The working hours seem to get longer and the line between the haves and the have-nots has become more distinct. In California, the 40-hour week with extra pay for overtime is a disputed legislative issue, and salaried employees are expected to work as many hours as it takes to get the job done.

The haves

On the have side, there are salaried employees who work for *avant-garde* firms who have all of the extra privileges for employees and their families: day care in the company, job sharing, maternity leave for either parent, health insurance, dental insurance, vision insurance, 401K's, and paid vacations.

The have-nots

On the have-not side, are the people who lost their permanent jobs through downsizing. Some now work as independent contractors, i.e. for themselves, trading independence for servitude. That means that they no longer have paid benefits, insurance, vacations. If they are not independent contractors, then they may be temporary employees. A recent PBS special on the city of San Diego clearly showed the demarcation. The temp workers find themselves in jobs just up to the point where the company will have to keep them permanently or let them go, and then they lose their jobs and begin all over again.

More and more families are without health insurance. More and more mothers and fathers find themselves putting in twelve-hour workdays because they are working for salary; and if they don't meet the requirements of the company, the company will give the job to someone else. As temps, they work extra hours to please with the expectation they may be

rewarded with a permanent job. When they are "laid off" instead, or their contract is terminated, they begin the pattern again with a new temporary job: hope, expectation, disappointment, cycle after cycle!

No protection

We have euphemized our language to de-emphasize the pain: "down-sized," "laid-off," instead of fired and discarded. Unions came into being to protect workers against abuse. They were effective. Now there is a stigma attached to being a blue-collar worker, to being unionized. That benefits the companies and hurts the individuals. Both Boeing and world trade protestors drew attention to Seattle in 1999. The union at Boeing came out of a sixteen-hour negotiation with this win: The company cannot require them to work extra weekend shifts without paying overtime. When world leaders met in Seattle in December of 1999, they were shocked by the American protestors who wanted to halt the departure of industrial jobs of the "working" man and woman from the United States. Where do people go if they are not educated and trained to move with the technological advances of our American society?

Downsized expectations

Who will represent and who will bargain for the workers who don't have a union? How many families today have the expectation that they will take a two-week paid vacation and go somewhere? How many families expect to spend long summer evenings in the back yard playing ball and talking with the neighbors. How many families would have time to use a front porch if they had one? Parents pick their children up from day care, stop at the supermarket or a fast food place, throw some food on the table, put the children to bed, and then fall asleep exhausted, knowing they'll have just a few hours of rest before they begin their early-morning roller coaster again.

A nation of nibblers

One Sunday edition of the *Orange County Register* bore this headline on the front page: "America Has Become a Nation of Nibblers."[6] I don't know about you, but I expect important news in the headlines on the front page: wars, plagues, disasters, victories. Unless you are in the fast food business, this is bad news for nutrition and for the American family. We are eating more in the car. Fast food restaurants encourage this with nibble-size menu items. It supports the pattern of life on the run.

The rat race

As fewer and fewer homes have two parents to share the burden of raising and feeding a family, in addition to the burden of "just getting by," of "making ends meet," individuals carry the burden of guilt because they're not really doing anything as well as they would like or think they should. Women stick with the family because they feel the guiltiest. If it didn't work out, there must be something they did wrong. People resent other people just because they "have a life." This is what Bob Kiyosaki in his book, *Rich Dad, Poor Dad,*[7] typifies as the rat race. We are like rats in a maze, "making ends meet," and so bound up in it that we can't step back from the drama of the situation to get it under control, to give ourselves space for change.

Getting and spending

I will use myself as an example. My children are grown and gone. I know I can best serve myself by arising early each morning and setting aside the best part of my day for writing. This is when my mind is clear, when the phone doesn't ring, when I can be creative and expressive, without interruption. Yet for years I put myself in a position where I took jobs that required early morning hours, when I had to be places and do things early in the morning, making it impossible for me to use the best time for the best work. It became as Wordsworth observes in "The World Is Too Much With Us": "Getting and spending we lay waste our powers/ Little we see in Nature that is ours./ We have given our hearts away, a sordid boon!"

Nose to the grindstone

It was easy for me to justify the early morning hours, the job that made the income I needed to survive, but it was strangling my spirit and misdirecting my energy. The activity came out fear, fear there wouldn't be enough, fear that if I left a gap, nothing might come to fill it, fear that I had to grab on to this fill-in job to "make ends meet." That is a race consciousness *old saying*, "to make ends meet." It suggests that we might barely be able to put enough together, but there will never be more than enough. The perceived need to "make ends meet" becomes a self-fulfilling prophecy. When you barely "make ends meet," the activity becomes an end in itself. It does not stretch outward or inward. It goes nowhere. When ends are meeting, there is no horizon. In order to "make ends meet," one must "stick one's nose to the grindstone," another *old saying*. Examine that image. With the nose attached to the grindstone, there is no looking up, no looking out, only mindless repetitious activity.

Confused and afraid

Most Americans are working so hard because they have goals to achieve. Yet, when we come at our own experience from scarcity thinking, with the thought that there isn't quite enough, then it is difficult for us to have faith that what we expect, what we wish, what we entertain in our heart of heart can really come true. This is called confusion. On the one hand we may set goals based on dreams; but on the other hand, we are saying that the goals are unachievable and that the dreams are pie in the sky. An object, for instance a car, cannot travel in two directions at the same time. We wouldn't even attempt it. Yet, how often do we live our life in such a way that the "push me-pull me" is constantly at war on our spirit. It reminds me of the farm boy who was drafted in the army. The sergeant was putting them through a drill, "Forward march," "Rear march," "Forward march," "Rear march." The boy went over and sat down. The sergeant asked, "Just what do you think you're doing?" The boy replied, "I ain't doin' nothin' until you make up your mind what you're doin'."

From the garage door to the front porch

You can probably tell that I still have "energy" around this part of my sentence. As we explore Fuller's concepts, however, we will find that if we let go of false life-savers, "piano tops," use leverage and synergy effectively, know our big picture, and set our navigation path, we can begin to get out of the rat race. We can move into a position of control over our lives, over our destiny. It can take us from the garage door to the front porch.

If "making ends meet" is a ruling force of your daily life, controls your actions, acknowledge it right here and right now. Also acknowledge that you have the ability, one step at a time, to take control, to move into the center, to direct your daily traffic, to reign sovereign over your state.

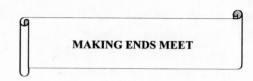

MAKING ENDS MEET

The areas in my life where I presently feel most stress are:

Job:

_____

_____

_____

_____

_____

Money:

_____

_____

_____

_____

_____

Children
Quality time:

Child Care:

Parents:

I nurture myself by:

My greatest fear is:

_____

_____

_____

_____

When I feel afraid, I deal with my fear by:

_____

_____

_____

_____

_____

"My children," said an old man to his boys scared by a figure in the dark entry, "my children, you will never see anything worse than yourselves." As in dreams, so in the scarcely less fluid events of the world every man sees himself in colossal, without knowing that it is himself. The good, compared to the evil which he sees, is as his own good to his own evil.

Emerson, Spiritual Laws [1]

Crime and punishment grow out of one stem. Punishment is a fruit that unsuspected ripens within the flower of the pleasure that concealed it. Cause and effect, means and ends, seed and fruit, cannot be severed; for the effect already blooms in the cause, the end preexists in the means, the fruit in the seed.

Emerson, Compensation [2]

Inherent Evil

Witness the black veil

Nathanial Hawthorne, one of the early articulators of the American Puritanism, may not have intended to make us scared of ourselves, but he certainly has that effect on me. In Hawthorne's story "The Minister's Black Veil," a young minister begins to wear a black crepe veil over his face. It becomes his emblem, his identity. He refuses to take it off for anyone, even his fiancée. The veil never changes, but the reaction of his observers has a curious evolution. At first the people in the village and in his congregation regard it with horror and revulsion. Then they become attracted to it, even obsessed with it. People come from far away to witness the black veil, and those on their deathbed wait to die for the minister with his veil to appear. Just before the minister's own death, another pastor suggests that he remove the veil, saying, "Before the veil of eternity be lifted, let me cast aside this black veil from your face!"

"Never!" cries out the minister, "On earth, never!"[3]

The condemnation

Hawthorne tells us the "black veil hung down, awful, at that last moment, in the gathered terrors of a lifetime." In his dying words, the minister speaks forth his condemnation upon all mankind:

'Tremble also at each other! Have men avoided me, and women shown no pity, and children screamed and fled, only for my black veil? What, but the mystery which it obscurely typifies, has

30

made this piece of crape so awful? When the friend shows his inmost heart to his friend; the lover to his best beloved; when man does not vainly shrink from the eye of his Creator, loathsomely treasuring upon the secret of his sin; then deem me a monster for the symbol beneath which I have lived and die. I look around me, and, lo! On every visage a Black Veil!"[4]

For one of my Introduction to Literature classes, I bought some black crepe fabric and cut it into veils. The students were divided into two groups and took turns wearing the veil and speaking with a partner. They found that when they wore the veil, they felt power, control, intimidation over the other person. It felt as if their eyes could penetrate into the hearts of the unveiled. Those without the veil felt uneasy, anxious, as if there were a darkness in their secret life that perhaps they hadn't yet revealed even to themselves. It was eerie. It is reminiscent of the popular radio program many years ago, *Suspense.* Those of you old enough will recall its lead opening, with the squeaking door followed by the sinister voice asking: "What evil lurks in the mind of men: Only the Shadow knows."

Young Goodman Brown
Lost Faith

In yet another story, Hawthorne takes "Young Goodman Brown" out into the forest. Young Goodman Brown is a fine, respected citizen, newly married to his lovely wife, Faith. He leaves Faith at home when he goes into the forest, for there he meets the Devil, his guide, dressed much as himself but carrying a staff that is a black serpent. Deep within the forest, he and the Devil meet the inhabitants. To his surprise, he finds the people of his village, those whom he regarded as the most upright of citizens, even Goody Cloyse who taught him catechism. There he even finds his wife, Faith, in her ribbons, and shocked to find her at such a cabal. He utters, "My Faith is gone!"

Hawthorne tells us at this awful moment, Young Goodman Brown looked into the horror of the human soul: "The whole forest was peopled with frightful sounds–the creaking of the trees, the howling of wild beasts, and the yell of Indians; while sometimes the wind tolled like a distant church bell, and sometimes gave a broad roar around the traveler, as if all Nature were laughing him to scorn. But he was himself the chief horror of the scene, and shrank not from its other horrors."[5] None escape.

The Devil

The Devil speaks his message:

'This night it shall be granted you to know their secret deeds: how hoary-hearted elders of the church have whispered wanton words to the young maids of their households; how many a woman, eager for widows' weeds, has given her husband a drink at bedtime and let him sleep his last sleep in her bosom; how beardless youths have made haste to inherit their father's wealth; and how fair damsels–blush not, sweet ones–have dug little graves in the garden, and bidden me, the sole guest, to an infant's funeral. By the sympathy of your human hearts for sin ye shall scent out all the places whether in church, bed-chamber, street, field, or forest–where crime has been committed, and shall exult to behold the whole earth one stain of guilt, one mighty blood spot. Far more than this. It shall be yours to penetrate, in every bosom, the deep mystery of sin, the fountain of all wicked arts, and which inexhaustibly supplies more evil impulses than human power—than my power at its utmost—can make manifest in deeds.'[6]

Hawthorne asks, "Had Goodman Brown fallen asleep in the forest and only dreamed a wild dream of a witch-meeting?" If it were so, it was "a dream of evil omen for young Goodman Brown. A stern, a sad, a darkly meditative, a distrustful, if not a desperate man did he become from the night of that fearful dream." And if it were a dream, is it any less real than waking up and finding yourself a cockroach?

Nothing changed

Deep in the American psyche is this race consciousness of inherent evil, which Hawthorne articulates, symbolized by the black veil, by the dark forest where we hide our sinful selves. Hawthorne published "Young Goodman Brown" in 1835 and "The Minister's Black Veil" in 1837. Note how the "sins" described in the witch meeting not only prevail but are media blitzes today: imposition of sexual advances by men in power positions on vulnerable young women; induction of early death by family members or care givers; murder to inherit wealth; abortion. A President was impeached for failing to admit sexual dalliance with a young woman in the oval office. A woman called "the gypsy" was arrested after the sudden death of the fifth husband to die under similar circumstances, each husband wealthy and 40-50 years older. A high school counselor was recently indicted for giving abortion information to a student. Dr. Kavorkian testified on his own behalf in his trial for performing self-assisted suicides. The circumstances are the same. We speak of these situations today as problems to be dealt with by law or prison or by redefinition of ethical standards. Yet, Hawthorne would tell us we are all in prison already; for on every visage is the black veil.

Collective guilt

In the race consciousness of guilt held collectively in our unconscious, these are the sins of the father visited on the son, our inheritance. We can shrug them off intellectually, but psychologically, emotionally, they have a grip. Note how Hawthorne makes us *voyeurs*, on the outside peering into the evil of others, passing judgment, condemning, denouncing, ostracizing. Sin becomes something God concocted for us, a cruel joke played out and executed by Satan. It is difficult to release this emotionally-charged vision of reality when evil has manifested, apparently without conscience, too frequently in mass events.

Assault of horror and tragedy

We still are not healed as a planet from the Holocaust. How can we heal when the wounds are re-opened with a fresh assault, and it seems as if the race consciousness and the "climate of opinion" have joined together in yet another and then another articulation of horror? We hear it on the radio, watch it in the news, in a mass murder of attorneys in San Francisco and of brokers in Atlanta, Georgia; in the Columbine High School massacre in Littleton, Colorado; in shootings at a Jewish day-care center in Los Angeles. Although statistically violent crime performed by juveniles is declining, our climate of opinion, however, is determined by what the media chooses to show us. The media is relentless in its coverage of mass tragedies and celebrates anniversaries with replays. In looking back over 1999 and its anniversary re-visits to mass violence, Matt Lauer, host of the CBS *Today Show*, was provoked to ask what role the media is playing in the promotion of an idea that then finds expression. Even though what we think to be true and what is, indeed, true may be two different things, as we think, however, we believe.

No money in good news

We can balance the Columbine High School tragedy with the publication of *The Freedom Writers Diary*, an anthology of accounts written by Wilson High School students in Long Beach, California. These students were all potential dropouts, unsupported at home and living on the fringe. They were turned around by a teacher, Erin Gruwell. In *The Freedom Writers Diary* these students, all high school graduates, tell about how they have overcome the abuses of their childhood and found hope from hardship, from a father who sold the family home to buy crack to a grandfather who molested his granddaughter.

These students received $250,000 from John Tu of Kingston Technology in Fountain Valley, California, the entrepreneur who has twice distinguished himself by sharing enormous bonuses with his employees. He supported the Tolerance Tour to Europe for this group of young men and women, and the group is supposed to have been considered as the subject of a Spielberg movie. Did this achievement by the students and their teacher receive equal time with Columbine? Alas, certainly not! Good news doesn't sell.

Laying blame

When something horrible occurs, we search for someone to blame. Columbine's atrocities were blamed on the videos the killers watched. Yet millions of people have watched the same videos and have not murdered anyone. There lurks in our consciousness both the assumption and the fear that we all have inherited a disposition for evil that might be awakened if we let down our guard. Our climate of opinion on the one hand, invokes the sanctity of childhood, the purity of children, the redemptive ability of the unspoiled human spirit that may momentarily be misdirected. On the other hand, our climate of opinion celebrates deviance and depravity. When I was growing up, people used to say that the worst thing that could happen to a juvenile delinquent was to get caught. In fact, here again the language expresses the climate of opinion. An adult killer is a criminal; a killer who is a child is a juvenile delinquent, one who left the path. It was thought that exposure of the juvenile to the criminal justice system with "hard criminals" would corrupt the juvenile even further.

Scared Straight

A revival, a second take, of a documentary made in the '70s was broadcast on MTV: *Scared Straight*. This was made by lifers in prison to show prison life for what it really is, to scare young kids caught for the first time into going straight. The director of this documentary, Arnold Shapiro, reports that although they do not have formal studies or hard data to show the effect of the first version of the film, they do have the letters written by parents and by teenage first offenders attesting to the power of the message. They were "scared straight."

In our Columbine and Wilson High School examples, we are confronted with two groups of children, one group from respectable families who express the most incredible evil; and another group who have been subjected to unspeakable abuse, yet who not only overcome it, but also triumph over it. Underlying both instances, however, is the recognition that the propensity for evil exists in the human spirit, waiting to be let out, a bad seed.

The angel in the stone

The story is told, perhaps apocryphal, that one day a gentleman was observing Michelangelo hacking away at a huge piece of stone. The gentleman said to him, "What are you doing?" To that query Michelangelo replied, "I'm releasing an angel." There is an angel in each one of us, a pattern of perfection. It is often a struggle to focus on the angel when we are surrounded by voices of those who focus on the devil. In Milton's *Paradise Lost*, when Satan, a mighty and egotistical angel, has been defeated in his attempt to overcome God, he and his troop of followers, the fallen angels, land abruptly in the very pit of Hell. An enormous hiss goes up from the depths as they all become snakes:

> They felt themselves now changing; down their arms,
> Down fell both spear and shield, down they as fast,
> And the dire hiss renewed, and the dire form
> Catched by contagion, like in punishment,
> As in their crime. Thus was the applause they meant
> Turned to exploding hiss triumph to shame
> Cast on themselves from their own mouths.
> *Paradise Lost*, x, 541-547

The "climate of opinion" hisses around us.

From acorn to tree

We know the tiny acorn within the shell contains within it the essence of beingness of the tree, is the truth of the tree within the seed. In the course of growing down, putting out roots, then growing up, putting forth branches, the tree is subjected to the vicissitudes of nature, to variations of light and dark, water and drought, cold and warmth. The truth of the being of that tree is pre-determined, but the climate changes. The tree in becoming who it is must learn to deal with the climate, must adapt. It never deviates from its self-knowledge, but all of its self-knowledge may not be expressed if the demands of the environment do not require it.

Self-knowingness

Our human path here is much the same. Our spirit knows itself, knows the truth of itself. Yet it is born into a climate of opinion that is forever changing and adapting, forever sending forth messages which may be true or may be false, but they have an effect on us. The message from our Puritan ancestry into which we were born tells us that man's inherent proclivity for evil makes suffering inevitable, that our goodness will only be as good as our ability to overcome temptation, that our life here on earth is meant to be a trial, that only the afterlife is of importance, and that the life we live here is lived for the hereafter rather than for the present. In fact, to be concerned with the present is self-indulgent.

Our choice

If we accept this thinking, we may find it hard to get out of bed in the morning. What is the point? As we will find when we begin to explore Fuller's ideological framework, we cannot "change one iota of yesterday." I accept that I carry around Hawthorne, the race consciousness, the climate of opinion created by the media. Yet, I am still at choice. I can choose to direct my attention to God's goodness and love. I can choose to focus on the angel in the stone. I can choose to nurture my mind and spirit with positive thoughts, with inspirational words, with acts of courage and kindness, with people who demonstrate purpose and direction. It may be a simple thing like playing a tape in the car rather than listening to the news or talk radio, reading with a child, stopping by to visit a friend, participating in a community project, or even taking my dog for a walk. We can choose whether to have a heavy heart or the joy that "passeth understanding." We choose in our minds, as Milton observes:

> A mind not to be changed by place or time.
> The mind is its own place, and in itself
> Can make a Heaven of Hell, a Hell of Heaven.
> *Paradise Lost*, 1, 254-256

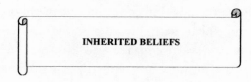

INHERITED BELIEFS

I never thought about things like race consciousness or climate of opinion, yet when I think about it, here are some of the ideas I just took for granted:

People who were poorer than I were:

_____

_____

_____

_____

People who were richer than I were:

_____

_____

_____

_____

People who were dumber than I were:

_____

_____

_____

_____

_____

People who were smarter than I were:

_____

_____

_____

_____

People who had different colored skin were:

_____

_____

_____

People who didn't talk as I talked were:

_____

_____

_____

There were certain people I was not supposed to talk to because:

_____

_____

_____

I did *or didn't* go to church because:

_____

_____

_____

I thought if I did something bad, I would be punished by:

_____

_____

_____

I thought God looked like:

_____

_____

I thought the devil looked like:

_____

_____

_____

_____

Nothing seems so easy as to speak and to be understood. Yet a man may come to find that the strongest of defenses and of ties–that he has been understood; and he who has received an opinion may come to find it the most inconvenient of bonds.

Emerson, Spiritual Laws [1]

Ah, but a man's reach should exceed his grasp,
Or what's a heaven for?

Robert Browning, Andrea del Sarto ll. 97-98

For thence,—a paradox
Which comforts while it mocks,
Shall life succeed in that it seems to fail:
What I aspired to be,
And was not, comforts me:
A brute I might have been, but would not sink I' the scale.

Robert Browning, Rabbi Ben Ezra, ll. 38-43

Limits: Living Someone Else's Idea

First adolescent love

In *Dubliners* James Joyce tells a poignant story of adolescent puppy love, "Araby." The speaker in the story has just discovered that he prefers watching out the window for his friend, Mangan's, older sister than playing with his friends in the blind alley where their homes are located: "Her name sprang to my lips at moments in strange prayers and praises which I myself did not understand. My eyes were often full of tears (I could not tell why) and at times a flood from my heart seemed to pour itself out into my bosom. I thought little of the future. I did not know whether I would ever speak to her or not or, if I spoke to her, how I could tell her of my confused adoration. But my body was like a harp and her words and gestures were like fingers running upon the wires."[2]

The young damsel, aware of the attention, plays with the boy when she encounters him from her front porch. "She asked me was I going to Araby. I forgot whether I answered yes or no. It would be a splendid bazaar, she said she would love to go." As she speaks, she twists her silver bracelet "round and round her wrist. She could not go, she said, because there would be a retreat that week in her convent." He promises that if he goes, he will bring her something.

Temptation to quest

It becomes the boy's obsession to go to Araby to buy her a gift. The very name of "Araby" evokes all that is exotic and romantic. On the designated day, his uncle's payday, he waits in pain for the money for his train ride to Araby. It gets later and later; and when his uncle finally comes home, a true Dubliner, he has been drinking and makes coarse jokes. The boy rushes out of the house, gets on the train, and arrives at Araby only to find it closing down: "I recognized a silence like that which pervades a church after a service." The boy frantically looks for a gift, finding he hasn't enough money to buy anything. He stops at a stall and interrupts a young man and woman engaged in love talk. She asks him if he wishes to buy something. "The tone of her voice was not encouraging." He looks at the "great jars that stood like eastern guards at either side of the dark entrance to the stall and murmured, 'No, thank you.'" As he walks away, he "allowed the two pennies to fall against the sixpence in my pocket." As he leaves, Joyce tells us, "Gazing up into the darkness I saw myself as a creature driven and derided by vanity; and my eyes burned with anguish and anger."

The humiliation of failure

This is the mature James Joyce observing his adolescent self, recalling the bitter memory of this impotent moment. Mangan's sister is long gone in real life, probably married with twelve children, but she is seared into Joyce's memory. How many of us have attempted to bring a gift from Araby to someone who long ago forgot she ever mentioned wanting it? How many of us have returned over and over to Araby, seeking the extraordinary, humiliated by our failure, acting out a pattern of behavior for which the initial cause long ago evaporated? In the subtle exchange of communication, whether sensualized and eroticized, as for Joyce, or whether accepted by one in a subordinate position from one in control, the desire to please and satisfy someone else may impose limits for a lifetime. We may keep acting out someone else's dream and never come up with our own. This is a familiar pattern in adolescence, and many of us never graduate and grow up.

Must and should

In my work with people, I have discovered that the more developed the ego function, the more obligations and responsibilities take the forefront, the more "must" and "should" enter their vocabularies. We make a distinction, however, between the self-defining and self–empowering fulfillment of obligations and responsibilities and the fulfillment of the obligations and responsibilities repeated again and again with no *apparent* inner logic. In the latter instance, one may be acting out of some felt need to respond to some distant message, long ago forgotten by the messenger. It may, in fact, have been a passing, incidental expression of the messenger that was then taken to heart by the recipient, blown out of proportion, and elevated to serve as a *raison d'etre*. Mangan's sister forgot about Araby long ago. James Joyce, as a mature adult is still going there. As Emerson says "He who has received an opinion may come to find it the most inconvenient of bonds."

Rage for order

The physicist Heisenberg noted that in the process of any interaction, in scientific observation, the observer is linked to the object being observed, and the object is altered by the process of the observation. To carry this insight into our every-day activities and affairs, we must say that in the process of even the most brief of conversations, the listener and the speaker are altered by the connection. Do we have any desire in life greater than to understand and to be understood?

There is a drive for order, for the system to be working effi-ciently, for the organism to be in harmony and peace. As human beings, we are highly complex organisms. When one part of the organism is in disharmony, is not functioning effi-ciently, the whole organism rushes to that place to repair, to take care, to re-establish the *status quo*. Physically, our bodies are programmed to do this. When we cut ourselves, the organ-ism repairs the wound, fills it back up, covers it over. We do not have to say to our bodies, this is what we want to happen. Our bodies know.

The subliminal message

Our minds react similarly. When we are confused, we are ill at ease, nervous. We use words such as "wander" to describe the state of confusion; because when we are confused, we lack direction. We lose a sense of who we are, and we do not know where we are going. As we learn, we experience temporary confusion, a time when our minds are groping to put together a myriad of impulses and ideas and to re-organize them into a state that we can comprehend. We grow as we grope for com-prehension, seeking the re-organization of data into an under-standable context.

In the same way, we seek to be understood, we seek to com-municate our entire beings. If words are only seven percent of communication, the auditory sound of our voices fifty-five percent, and our body language thirty-eight percent, then in a conversation the exchange that is taking place is an actual exchange of essence, of aura, of energy fields. When Mangan's sister twirls her bracelet, she sexualizes her desire to go to Araby, and the boy is aroused subconsciously, not consciously aware. She knows what she is doing; she plays with him. We know when we have been understood, when we have been heard, when we have been felt, when we have been seen. A child quickly learns to understand the message of the parent, articulated or not. The child knows not only what acceptable behavior is, but also how the child stands in relation to the parent.

The parents' messages

For much of my life, I was acting out my parents' messages. Just as the son in "The Judgment" saw his sickly father as a "giant of a man," so did I perceive my parents. My mother was, and is still at 84, a very pretty woman. She has always spent what seems like hours each day primping and making herself more pretty. One of my earliest memories is of a Luzier representative, an early Mary Kay, coming to our house and selling my mother cosmetics over the kitchen table. As I write this the smell of my mother from my childhood comes back to me. No one was supposed to be more pretty than mother. That included me. My father was a very smart man. He prided himself on his ability to think, to know, and to solve problems. He had a photographic memory and could synthesize information effectively. No one was supposed to be smarter than my father. One could be smart, for that would be a reflection of him in me, but one could not be smarter.

Knowing the limits

So mother would dress me up as her little doll. She made me sit still every night so that she could set my hair in long curls. Often she would dress me in an outfit like hers, having matching outfits custom-made for us. She always looked better in them than I did. Those were the rules. In my mind, it was acceptable to look good, but not better. It was acceptable to be bright, but not brighter. One could be oneself up to a point, but one could not exceed that point, for it was reserved for the parent. Those were my limits.

When I attended elementary school, I was a very smart little girl. The teachers and students all acknowledged that. Also, I was a leader. Although I was chubby, I was elected as a cheerleader and even had a boyfriend. Because I had enough to eat, enough to wear, and a sense of achievement, I thought that I was ok. It did not seem strange and unusual to me that each week I had three clean dresses. I would wear one on Monday, another on Tuesday, and the third on Wednesday. Then I could choose two of the three to wear a second time on Thursday and Friday.

Since this was the way we did things at our house, and since I was always clean, this is how I thought life was supposed to be. Mother would come to visit on parent-visitation day, and the children would say to me, "Your mother is so pretty. It's too bad you don't look like her." And I would know that both at school and at home, mother was prettier. My principal had been my father's teacher in elementary school, and she considered my father the most brilliant student she ever had. So I knew my limit: I could be smart, but not so smart as my father.

Acting the limits out

When I left elementary school, I went to a junior high that brought together students from four elementary schools: Lincoln, Jefferson, McKinley, and Garfield. You can see that my community was strong on presidential leadership. There I discovered that McKinley and Jefferson, the two elementary schools I had attended, were both on the "wrong side of the tracks." Where I had been "good enough" but not better than my parents at McKinley, now I wasn't even "good enough." My boyfriend already had a girlfriend from Garfield, and I was just an overweight, badly dressed, smart but outcast girl from McKinley. Because our sixth grade teacher, Mrs. Kauffman, had taught us to stand and recite, I continued to do that in my classes. Finally, Miss Bierlein, in my seventh grade math class, told me that it wasn't necessary to stand. I felt completely humiliated.

There was nowhere to go but inside. My outer self was disconnected from my inner self. I didn't understand, and I certainly was not understood. The only place I could find harmony and peace was in the imagination, in books, and I spent all of my time reading. My mother resented my reading. She constantly said to me, "Get your nose out of that book." Yet when the study hall teacher came to look at an apartment we had for rent, and when she told my mother that I had the highest achievement scores in the seventh grade, then mother determined that I must be first and stay first. I was caught in a constant state of confusion because I was supposed to get my nose out of the book, yet I was supposed to be first, which meant that I had to have my nose in a book. But my father was first, so how could I be first?

Unintentional messengers

I am sharing this with you because, in retrospect, I realize that my parents were just being themselves. The messages I integrated into my emotional and intellectual life were the ones I interpreted, absorbed, and acted upon. I did it. They didn't. Yet I am like James Joyce, in maturity observing my adolescent self. It takes us back to the sentencing. The limits we place on ourselves are of our own making, our own acceptance of messages often delivered quite without deliberation and intent by the deliverer who was just being himself.

Self sabotage

I won't burden you with an inventory of the times in my life that I have acted upon my perceived limits, some seemingly incongruent self-sabotage to keep me from being first or best. As I consider this, it makes sense of something that happened right after I was married at the age of 22. I had completed both a B.A. and M.A. from the University of Michigan, putting myself through school with scholarships and part-time jobs. My new husband proceeded right after the wedding to make me get rid of my clothes. The words "make me" today give me a shudder, but then they were a part of my vocabulary. I had dressed a little exotically. Those were the "beatnik" days, and I carried a green book bag and wore black tights. Most of my clothes were purchased by my mother "on sale," and she had an eye for the unusual. I remember in particular two extraordinary, quilted full skirts. One was purple with large, brilliantly colored flowers and the other was black with large gold coin-shaped dots. I loved wearing those skirts, and I recall that I had a fitted black coat to wear over them.

When my husband started getting rid of my clothes, it didn't even occur to me that how I dressed must have, in part, attracted him to me. I didn't express a single word of indignation. In retrospect, looking back at this still adolescent self from a standpoint of maturity, I realize that his message to me was clearly that I wasn't good enough. I sought out someone who would give me that message so that I could stay within my self-imposed limit, so that I could fulfill *my sentence.*

Sentences generalized

This ability to self-sabotage as we fulfill *our sentence* may manifest in the financial realm as well. Frequently a pattern will emerge for an individual who achieves a level of income almost as high as his parents'. When the income is about to exceed the parents' level, he does something to get himself demoted or fired, some self-defeating act, a self-sabotage, because unconsciously he fears being better than, or outdoing his parents. The message that individual took in from his parents is that he is not to be better. It may be that the parents never consciously meant to send that message, but they were acting out, living out their own response to *their sentence* in life.

For many of us living out a life sentence, living out someone else's dream, or living out someone else's limits, may be strangling our ability to move forward in our own lives. We will be exploring "piano tops" in our discussion of Fuller's concepts. When we cling to "piano tops," we are hanging on to a lifesaver that has ceased to serve us effectively.

You may ask yourself at this point whether the dream you have for the unfolding of your life originates in you, or whether you got it from someone else. When you talk to yourself, is it your voice or someone else's? How did you come to formulate, to own, your vision for your life? If it isn't yours, what must you change for you to make it your own?

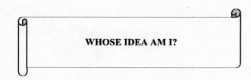

WHOSE IDEA AM I?

My earliest childhood dreams for myself came from many places: stories, movies, comic books, radio and television shows. As I remember those dreams, they were:

_____

_____

_____

_____

_____

When I played games with other children, like school, or theater, or doctor, the part I wanted to play was:

_____

_____

_____

_____

_____

_____

When people asked me what I wanted to be when I grew up, I said:

_____

_____

_____

_____

_____

_____

_____

This is what I really was thinking when they asked that question:

_____

_____

_____

_____

_____

_____

_____

I knew that when my parents asked that question, this is the answer they expected:

_____

_____

_____

_____

_____

_____

I still remember when I couldn't do what my first boy/girl friend wanted me to do:

_____

_____

_____

_____

_____

The first time I really felt disappointed with myself that I can remember is:

_____

_____

_____

_____

_____

For, what with my whole world-wide wandering,
      What with my search drawn out thro' years, my hope
      Dwindled into a ghost not fit to cope
With that obstreperous joy success would bring,
I hardly tried now to rebuke the spring
      My heart made, finding failure in its scope.

Robert Browning, Childe Roland to the Dark Tower Came ll. 19-24

Tho' much is taken, much abides; and tho'
We are not now that strength which in old days
Moved earth and heaven, that which we are, we are,—
One equal temper of heroic hearts,
Made weak by time and fate, but strong in will
To strive, to seek, to find, and not to yield.

Tennyson, Ulysses, ll. 66-71

Too Easy: The Oxen And The Eagle

> Each man has his own vocation. The talent is the call. There is one direction in which all space is open to him. He has faculties silently inviting him thither to endless exertion. He is like a ship in a river; he runs against obstructions on every side but one, on that side all obstruction is taken away and he sweeps serenely over a deepening channel into an infinite sea.
>
> Emerson, "Spiritual Laws"[1]

Your boat

Successfully navigated?

Isn't that a great picture that Emerson paints for us? Here you are, cast in this mighty metaphor with a great emotional rush of freedom, confidence and self assurance, at the triumphant end of the movie, *This Is Your Life*, in full Technicolor, riding your little boat into the sunset, fully able to enter any port at any time and to have exactly what you need.

Wow! Or does the voice inside you say, "Oops, there's something wrong with this picture?" We talk of walking the road of life; we are pathfinders. It is one thing to be walking or finding, but it's quite another to just be sweeping through deep water into an infinite whatever. This infinite is unknown.

Out of control?

Does the voice inside of you say, "Wait a minute. How do I know I can stop when I need to? How do I know the boat won't get away from me? How do I know that this isn't a trick, a mistake? How do I know that I won't get off course. Haven't I heard all my life that if it's easy, it isn't worth doing?" Poets write poems about the importance of what's difficult.

Fit to fail?

In "Childe Roland to the Dark Tower Came," Robert Browning tells us that we must be fit to fail. That is how we must measure ourselves. We truly win when we open ourselves to the full possibility of failure. That is essential to run for any office, to compete in any event. There will be only one winner. Tennyson concludes "Ulysses" with the line most quoted in "Commencement" addresses, the quest of life: "To strive, to seek, to find, and not to yield." The underlying assumption is that we never quite reach the far goal. We know who we are from the big stretch, the achievement not quite realized. Browning sums it up when he admonishes us:

Far better to aim for 1000 and miss it by one,

Than to aim for 500 and make it.

Too easy

Emerson meant to instruct and to inspire us with this analogy of the boat sailing so easily; for he says that when we are doing the right work, following the right vocation, the path opens effortlessly before us. How easy is it to accept this inspiration? Your grandmother may have told you, "Little boats belong close to shore." This implies, "If you go out to sea, how will you get back?" The current runs toward the sea. Your little boat won't be able to navigate against the current to get back where you were. It's a total risk. Once you've moved with the flow, there's no returning to safety, to where you were.

Besides

Besides, if it's easy, it must not be important. Why
"besides?" Shakespeare put many of his most important statements in "asides." Did you ever notice how, when you speak of
the thing most important to you, you may interject a "Well,
besides?" Have you ever said such things as, "The weather's
really too lousy for us to go; besides, I don't have anything to
wear anyhow." Or have you ever said, "I don't know why I
overslept and missed the interview; besides, they wouldn't
have hired me anyway." When we say "besides," we are really
expressing the most important thing to us. "Besides, I don't
have anything to wear" really means, "I don't feel good about
the way I look in any of my clothes." "Besides, they wouldn't
have hired me anyway," really says, "I don't feel that I have the
qualifications I need to do the work I'd like to do." Often a
"besides" is a little cry from inside us that says either "I'm not
enough," or "I might not be enough."

Staying stuck

"Besides" indicates the fear of letting go, the fear of moving
beyond the obstacle, because the obstacle, the staying stuck is
familiar. We feel grounded in the marsh or the swamp, knowing that we might sink, but at least we won't be swept away. It
takes tremendous courage to do what's easy, apparent, and
comfortable; because when we do that, we take full responsibility for our little ship, our little self.

Adam and Eve: the first stuck

Being human is being stuck. That is one of those things I
learned on the front porch. It may have been as early as the

summer before the fourth grade when I went on the bus every morning to the Tabernacle Bible School. God set us up to be stuck. That is what original sin is all about. I eat apples, but I didn't eat *the apple*. Eve ate *the apple*, and ever since, we have all been stuck. Although I know that the writing of the first two books of Genesis was at least three centuries apart, when I go back to the first two chapters of Genesis, as a reader, not as a Biblical scholar, I feel set up. This is how I interpret the human condition described in the first two chapters of *Genesis*.

God-given dominion

When God has finished his work, when he has created man and woman in his own image, he speaks, "Let us make man in our image, after our likeness: and let them have dominion over the fish of the sea, and over the fowl of the air, and over the cattle, and over all the earth, and over every creeping thing that creepeth upon the earth." And then God blessed them and he said to them, "Be fruitful, and multiply, and replenish the earth, and subdue: and have dominion over the fish of the sea, and over the fowl of the air, and over every living thing that moveth upon the earth." This is the first chapter of *Genesis*. God repeats our dominion twice.

Not really

Then we come to the second chapter. God just gave us "dominion," and now he already takes it away. God, not man, determined to create hardship; for in the second chapter of *Genesis*, before God has made man, he does the planting of his Garden of Eden: "And the Lord God planted a garden eastward in Eden; and there he put the man whom he had formed. And out of the ground made the Lord God to grow every tree that is pleasant to the sight, and good for food; the tree of life also in the midst of the garden, and the tree of knowledge of good and evil."

God no longer direct

Suddenly God no longer "goes direct." He who spoke directly about creeping and flying and dominion now has Adam speak of the birth of Eve. It is Adam who states, "This is now bone of my bones and flesh of my flesh: she shall be called Woman, because she was taken out of man." God evades the issue that determines the entire future of man in his intercourse with other men. He puts it in the mouths of the serpent and the first woman, both acknowledged as God's creations. Indeed, we are told by some strange, unidentified, now omniscient speaker, "The serpent was more subtle than any beast of the field which the Lord God had made."

Eve and the serpent

Only when the serpent and Eve talk, do we learn of the consequences of eating of the tree in the middle of the garden, the "tree of knowledge of good and evil." However could it be that this serpent and this woman, newly made and introduced to life, could even conceive of death, of the knowing of good and evil? All of this is the creation of God. He planted the garden. God knows whom and what he has created, and he fully anticipates the results. He is waiting in the wings to condemn his creation for doing what he knew all along it would do.

Master and slave

This dilemma has plagued and delighted philosophers and theologians for centuries. Perhaps Hegel saw it most clearly when he determined that God from the beginning wanted a master and slave situation, wanted to be amused by the antics of man and pleased by his position of authority over man. The arguments for free will are a cruel joke we play on ourselves to explain the human condition, our rationalization of the trap laid for us.

Man's theistic rendering

The story in *Genesis* comes out of an oral tradition, not as the actual spoken word of God, but rather as the manifestation of man's attempt to define himself and to explain how he got the way he is. Man in the Bible creates God in the image and the likeness of himself. This is man's rendition of the way he thinks God spoke. He is a powerful father, somewhere up above, looking down and keeping score. Both stories in *Genesis* express an explanation arising from our race consciousness, evolved as man has evolved, a statement of why we must struggle in a universe that is so perfect in every way, and why man, more than any other creature, must be aware of this struggle, must be pulled apart by it in his mind and soul. We thrust the responsibility on a higher power; because if we must accept that responsibility for ourselves, we are crushed by our weakness, by our susceptibility to get ourselves into trouble.

Life is supposed to be difficult. How can it be not difficult?

How then can we be comfortable as a little ship flowing out into the ocean? Everything in our collective unconscious, everything in our primordial memory cries out against this ease. Life is difficult. I remember in my adolescence playing Debussy's *Arpeggios* when I took piano lessons. The nun, Sister Mary Paula, my teacher, had starched white cuffs against her small wrists. When I hear Mozart or Haydn, the image of those cuffs represents to me cleanliness, precision, clarity.

Sister Mary Paula told me to play the triplets against the eighth notes in the Debussy by saying, "Not difficult, not difficult, not difficult, not difficult." I can still hear the music of that phrase. Truthfully, the execution of this piece of music was difficult, but my mind took control of the situation, got my hands through it. Sometimes when I'm in the midst of a task that challenges me, I recite this musical phrase as an affirmation, as a touchstone: *not difficult*.

Fire and Ice.

Life is difficult. Survival is difficult. Hasn't the earth been ravaged by storms, by flood, by hail, by sleet, by fire, by ice. Man envisions the end of the planet as cataclysmic because the origin of the planet was cataclysmic. The planet emerged from a burst of energy, at once both creative and destructive. We carry this memory in our collective unconscious, at once knowing our origin and fearfully anticipating our end. "In the end is the beginning," says T. S. Eliot.

The poet Robert Frost says of "Fire and Ice":

> Some say the world will end in fire,
> Some say in ice.
> From what I've tasted of desire
> I hold with those who favor fire.
> But if it had to perish twice,
> I think I know enough of hate
> To say that for destruction ice
> Is also great
> And would suffice.[2]

The cataclysmic memory

Thus, no matter what language we speak, whether we read or write, whether we are poets or philosophers, slaves or kings, tradesmen or warriors, seamen or tillers of the field, there is within us the cataclysmic memory. This is the pain relived in childbirth. We may or may not choose to believe that the pain and fear came from eating the fruit of a forbidden tree. That depends upon one's theology. This memory, apart from any intellectual explanation, we share from an inner knowing, a consciousness so powerful that it is what truly distinguishes the human condition; for man alone among all creatures is able to articulate it and to share it in symbols and metaphors, in oxymorons, in paradoxes. In man alone the physical and the metaphysical become one.

Struggle familiar

And thus we cling to the familiar, to the known, because within us is the fear of the unknown. We cling to what is difficult, for in the struggle against it, we can feel defined; it gives us a grasp upon reality. We inherited the Judaic-Christian belief in struggle. As Americans, we got the Puritanical work ethic as well; and we are suspicious of anyone for whom life comes too easily.

Suffering punishment

We delight in hearing the horrors of the personal lives of people who express a natural talent. We expect our artists, writers, actors, and musicians to be "poor starving," because they can't expect to be paid if they love their work. I even recall a televised speech made in the '90's by President George Bush at a conference on education when he articulated the assumption, the inference that teachers shouldn't expect to make much money because they like what they do. We watch *Entertainment Tonight,* and we read the scandal-sheet headlines as we go through the supermarket. It reassures us that the life of the rich and famous is wracked with pain and torment: crooked face lifts, alcohol and drug rehab, gigantic weight gains, family rejection, spousal abuse. We watch Jerry Springer to see people more screwed up than we are. It justifies our chains, our submission to the yoke.

The oxen and the eagle

Man compares himself to the oxen in his metaphors, as often he compares himself to the bird. As Hamlet says in his soliloquy, his "aside," when he tells the truth of himself, "My mind flies up. My thoughts remain below." Man is the oxen and the eagle, planted in the earth, inheritor of its struggle, with a mind that can carry him above and beyond, back to the true origins of his oneness with the creative impulse. How then can we be comfortable with the image of ourselves as a little ship flowing freely out to sea, unobstructed by difficulty?

Rediscovery: out at sea

What if paradoxically, for man is a paradox, we were to acknowledge the other memory that took us millions of years, perhaps billions to *rediscover?* We have all along been riding on a ship that is hurtling through space, unobstructed. *Re dis cover* is a wonderful word. We *re,* do again, *dis,* undo, what somehow we had *cover* ed, that is, put under wraps, never removing, never destroying, only getting out of sight, that is, out of the light of knowing, what has been true all along. We begin our voyage now as we began, "our end is our beginning." Can it be the struggles, the obstacles are all in our minds? Changing your mind is only a thought away.

```
┌─────────────────────────────────────┐
│                                     │
│            EASY DOES IT             │
│                                     │
└─────────────────────────────────────┘
```

The thing I enjoyed doing most when I was a child was:

_____

_____

_____

_____

The contests I remember winning were:

_____

_____

_____

_____

I hated people who were good at things I couldn't do because:

_____

_____

_____

_____

The thing people have praised me most for is:

                    approval of
_____

_____

_____

When I got praised for my achievement, I would say:

_____

_____

_____

_____

It's hard for me to remember things I did right, but I remember screwing up these things:

_____

_____

_____

_____

When things are hard for me, then I feel:

_____

_____

_____

_____

If I could just do what I enjoy most, it would be:

_____

_____

_____

_____

_____

I always thought I couldn't make my living by what comes most easily to me because:

_____

_____

_____

_____

_____

_____

When I heard the learn'd astronomer,
When the proofs, the figures, were ranged in columns before me,
When I was shown the charts and diagrams, to add, divide, and measure
    them,
When I sitting heard the astronomer where he lectured with much
    applause in the lecture room,
How soon unaccountable I became tired and sick,
Till rising and gliding out I wander'd off by myself,
In the mystical moist night-air and from time to time,
Look'd up in perfect silence at the stars.
Walt Whitman, 1865

This world is not Conclusion.
A species stands beyond—
Invisible, as Music—
But positive, as Sound—
It beckons, and it baffles—
Philosophy—don't know—
And through a Riddle, at the last—
Sagacity, must go—
To guess it, puzzles scholars—
To gain it, Men have borne
Contempt of Generations
And Crucifixion, shown—
Faith slips—and laughs, and rallies—
Blushes, if any see—
Plucks at a twig of Evidence—
And asks a Vane, the way—
Much Gesture, from the Pulpit—
Strong Hallelujahs roll—
Narcotics cannot still the Tooth
That nibbles at the soul—
Emily Dickinson, 1862

Part 2: A Conceptual Framework

* We are all astronauts on a planet we understand by trial and error.

* We come at our knowledge in two ways:

  Physical: Observation of physical and mathematical laws;

  Metaphysical Mental application of observed and intuited perfection.

* We are links in the "Great Chain of Being," suspended watchers, seeking knowledge of perfection through intuited truth and rational analysis.

Having, then, made all these preparations, he did not wish to lose any time in putting his plan into effect, for he could not but blame himself for what the world was losing by his delay, so many were the wrongs that were to be righted, the grievances to be redressed, the abuses to be done away with, and the duties to be performed. Accordingly, without informing anyone of his intention and without letting anyone see him, he set out one morning before daybreak on one of those very hot days in July. Donning all his armor, mounting Rocinante, adjusting his ill-contrived helmet, bracing his shield on his arm, and taking up his lance, he sallied forth by the back gate of his stable yard into the open countryside. It was with great contentment and joy that he saw how easily he had made a beginning toward the fulfillment of his desire. Cervantes, *Don Quixote*[1]

We Are All Astronauts

Already an astronaut

If the idea of riding in Emerson's boat easily out to sea created anxiety, then just relax. You're already on board a ship easily and effortlessly traveling without obstruction. When R. Buckminster Fuller wrote his little book, *Operating Manual for Spaceship Earth*, he spoke of the planet we had not yet seen from the moon, awakening us so vividly to the visual and experiential awareness that we are all astronauts. Space travel is perfectly natural to us; we just didn't know it. We have all been taking for granted our sophisticated travel aboard this extraordinary vessel. As Fuller pointed out, we have been spinning and zipping through space at a speed only one-fourth less than that required for a rocket to launch into its own orbit

> Spaceship Earth was so extraordinarily well invented and designed that to our knowledge humans have been on board it for two million years not even knowing that they were on board a ship. And our spaceship is so superbly designed as to be able to keep life regenerating on board despite the phenomenon, entropy, by which all local physical systems lose energy. So we have to obtain our biological life-regenerating energy from another spaceship—the sun.[2]

Space exploration natural evolution

This casts a new light on our perception of our selves. We are participants in a great adventure, and we didn't even know it. Adventure is our natural state. No wonder we love it so much. One would expect us to create rockets to carry us to other planets, while hurtling through space on our own ship. Space exploration is part of our natural evolution, of our own self-discovery. Just as man emerged from the water, a great amphibian, as Loren Eiseley describes in *The Immense Journey*, struggling up on shore to take his first breath of air, the first intake of life to suit man to earth, so also is it equally as natural for man to move outward into space, where he has always been. We are the only creatures who don the appropriate gear to go down to the depth of the sea and then out into space to push back the frontier. We thought it, imagined it, long before we could do it. We make waves, and we make roads, not where they've always been, but rather where we want them to be.

The road of life

We in America have always been fascinated with the image of man on the road of life, at the edge of the frontier. It may be, in part, because, unless we're indigenous Americans, we all came from immigrant roots. Somewhere in our past is at least one individual who was an inveterate risk taker, willing to leave everything familiar, comfortable, and valued behind. That individual was willing to test himself against all odds. It took resilience, courage, fortitude, persistence, intelligence, and faith. Our American western features this kind of hero. John Ford, one of our greatest directors of western films, likes to put his hero, alone on the road of life, against the backdrop of Monument Valley, with vast mountains and canyons in the background, encountering trials to his survival instinct and tests to his moral virtue. Events force him to act decisively.

The wary, wily, savvy searcher and winner

The man on the frontier masters his challenges because he is wary, wily, and savvy. The environment and its inhabitants are his to conquer. The western celebrates visionaries who look at a wood and see a lumberyard, who look at a trail and see a railroad, who look at a river and see a dam. The challenge and the quest beckon this man forward, whether in a covered wagon seeking a homestead or on a mule with a grubstake searching for gold. Two of John Ford's westerns are appropriately entitled: *The Searchers* and *How the West Was Won*. Searching and winning are the American way and embody the American Dream.

Space: the next frontier

When the frontier, defined and depicted by the Western, was too earth-bound, too limited, George Lucas and Stephen Spielberg moved it outward into space. Spielberg humanized it with *ET*, and Lucas "westernized" it with the *Star Wars* series. The backdrop has changed to outer space, but the issues are the same: good over evil, courage over fear, intelligence over error, mastery over tools. When George Lucas re-released *The Star Wars Trilogy* as a single film production, more than a decade after the original films, taking advantage of improvements in sound and visual technology, it grossed seventeen million dollars the first weekend. *The Phantom Menace*, which takes us back in time before the *Star Wars Trilogy* created such anticipation that movie-goers waited in line for hours to get tickets and then slept outside the theaters the night before the opening. The sales of the video were unprecedented. What is the great fascination?

Primordial link to our human voyage

The attraction of the *Star Wars* story is its primordial link to our human voyage on our spaceship, to its re-enactment of our mythological quest for knowledge and understanding of how the power of the universe works and how the individual as one entity squares away a single life and fits into this paradigm. It is one man, capable of succeeding in the universe by trusting himself. Skywalker must defeat clearly defined evil, Darth Vadar. All the intention and mastery of the universe comes together in this moment of moral decision. Will it be the inhumanity and darkness of Darth Vadar, or will it be the victory of human purpose, of pure intention, of courageous action, the victory of heart?

The Force

When the voice of Ben Kenobi is heard by Skywalker at the crisis in the last battle, it says, "Turn off your computer, turn off your machine and do it yourself, follow your feelings, trust your feelings." Above, beyond any mechanism created by the human brain, the mind of man is linked with the One mind, and the One mind feels, has heart. Lucas calls it "The Force," defined as energy by Ben Kenobi: "The force is an energy field created by all living things. It surrounds us, it penetrates us, it binds the galaxy together." When Ben Kenobi says, "May *The Force* be with you," he is speaking of the power that binds together the hearts and mind and soul of humanity in a unified action of intention and integrity. Fuller would call this "Universe." I would call it God.

Humanity's united quest

The united quest of humanity on the planet is an expression of this force. It is what has led us to discover how things work, to move from being the product of an explosion to the creator of the explosion. It is the activity that has taken us from the observation of physical principles to the application of those principles metaphysically. It has empowered man to figure out that nothing in the universe exists except energy, that life itself and all matter in all of its expressions on our planet are nothing but energy: the plants, the rocks, the soil, the minerals, the ever-transforming water that covers two-thirds of the earth, constantly in flux between its form of vapor, liquid, and solid.

We have moved from the primitive man's wonder and fear of a flash of lightening in the sky, to the production of a spark by rubbing two sticks together, to the smashing of an atom to create a bomb of devastating destruction and a rocket powerful enough to thrust a space capsule of our fabrication outside the force of gravity that anchors our little planet and all of its passengers in orbit around the sun. Thus has man's voyage on his planet, his history as an astronaut, been spent in figuring out how his little spaceship works and how it fits within the universe it occupies.

Celestial ships: not just a dream

In perhaps the earliest work of science fiction, in the early 1600s, Johannes Kepler, about whom we will hear more in the chapter "Trial and Error," imagined the movement of our craft through space in *Somnium,* "The Dream." Since he knew that it was hard for people on earth to believe that the earth was rotating because they didn't feel the movement, in his "dream" he imagines a journey to the moon with the space travelers observing Earth rotating above them. He imagines the continents and the oceans. He said of his dreaming, "...in a dream one must be allowed the liberty of imagining occasionally that which never existed in the world of sense perception." He believed that one day there would be "celestial ships with sails adapted to the winds of heaven" navigating the sky, filled with explorers unafraid of the vastness of space.[3]

Explorers of an aged Universe

Here at the beginning of a new century, the Hubble telecope has been refurbished; its value is estimated at $3.8 billion. It is anticipated that as the Hubble peers into the whirlpool of gas and dust swirling at the heart of the galaxy 100 million light years away, as it measures the velocity, decades of theoretical work on how objects interact to shape the cosmos may need to be eliminated or revised. We may find, for instance, that some of the oldest stars in the heavens, believed to be fifteen to twenty billion years old by our classic methods of measurement, may in fact be older than the universe itself.

Time our measurement, not the Universe's

Most of us do not wake up each morning wondering how old the universe is. If we have questions, they tend to concern themselves with ourselves. What we really want to know is where we stand with the universe, who we are, and where we are going. Should we have to modify our theories, it will not be the first time. Indeed, our natural process for sorting things out has been codified and defined as our scientific method: hypothesis, experiment, observation, conclusion. Man used this procedure long before we had a name for it. This is how we make discovery. Although the Kansas State Board of Education may prefer not to allow the public schools to teach the theory of evolution, the Pope of the Roman Catholic Church has accepted the theory as a valid scientific explanation. The theory will hold until we come up with one that comes closer to the truth, closer to explaining the phenomena, the data we observe and analyze. We have grown enough in our understanding to know that our language is symbolic; it expresses our current truth, our present knowledge, explanation and comprehension of the perfection of a machine that always works. Today we know it will be revised. It has not always been so.

'Tis so much joy!' Tis so much joy!
If I should fail, what poverty!
And yet, as poor as I
Have ventured all upon a throw;
Have gained! Yes! Hesitated so
This side the victory!

Life is but life, and death but death!
Bliss is but bliss, and breath but breath!
And if, indeed, I fail,
At least to know the worst is sweet.
Defeat means nothing but defeat,
No drearier can prevail!

And if I gain,—oh, gun at sea,
Oh, bells that in the steeples be,
At first repeat if slow!
For heaven is a different thing
Conjecture, and waked sudden in,
And might o'erwhelm me so!

Emily Dickinson[1]

Our life is an apprenticeship to the truth that around every circle another can be drawn; that there is no end in nature, but every end is a beginning; that there is always another dawn risen on mid-noon and under every deep a lower deep opens.

Emerson, Circles,[2]

Trial And Error

Man in center

When the late Carl Sagan's *Cosmos* series on public television was presented in the late 1970's, not only did it open the world of physics and scientific discovery to generally educated but non-scientific lay people, but also it put into perspective the absolutely devastating blow delivered to man's image of himself by Copernicus' message of truth about the movement of earth and the planets. When primitive man looked up in the sky, he assumed, as well he might, that the sky was out there, and he was at the center

Ptolemy's universe

It seemed only appropriate that Ptolemy, the early astronomer who named the stars and made so many discoveries about them and their brightness, should corroborate man's central position. Ptolemy observed that the Earth is a sphere, predicted eclipses, and established a model for plotting the movement of the planets. He concluded from his investigation of the heavens that the Earth was the center of the universe and that everything else moved around the Earth. This assumption nourished and sustained a religious belief based upon the premise that man, the child of God, is the center of the universe, and that all living and non-living things on the planet extend downward from him, and all angelical and heavenly things extend upward from him.

Copernicus: upstart astrologer

It is little wonder that when Nicholas Copernicus, in 1543, published a different hypothesis, reducing the earth to just another planet circling around the sun, he was met with indignation, denunciation and censorship. He had to be in error. How dare he undermine man's estimation of his place in the universe and the work of the philosophers, theologians, and poets who had celebrated it. It was an outcry that would not die down. His "truth" was totally unacceptable. More than half a century after his discovery, in 1616, the Catholic Church put his work on a list of forbidden books. It stayed on that list until 1835. The denunciation was not limited to the Catholic Church. Martin Luther called Copernicus an "upstart astrologer."

When Johannes Kepler, born in 1571 in Germany, proved beyond a doubt that Copernicus' observation was sound, he softened the blow of his confirmation with this statement of understanding why the man-centered interpretation of the universe held power in man's explanation of his home for so many centuries: "It is therefore impossible that reason not previously instructed should imagine anything other than that the Earth is a kind of vast house with the vault of the sky placed on top of it; it is motionless and without it the Sun being so small passes from one region to another, like a bird wandering through the air."[3]

God and geometry

Kepler observed the planets move according to precise mathematical laws and noted the time for a planet to complete one orbit is proportional to the cube of its distance from the sun, i.e. the farther from the sun, the more slowly it moves. He concluded from his work that God and Geometry were one: "Geometry existed before the Creation. It is co-eternal with the mind of God. Geometry provided God with a model for the Creation…Geometry is God himself."[4] Kepler even anticipated Newton and gravity by suggesting that the planetary movement was similar to the working of magnetism. He concluded that the "celestial machine is to be likened not to a divine organism but rather to a clockwork…insofar as nearly all the manifold movements are carried out by means of a single, quite simple magnetic force, as in the case of a clockwork {where} all motions {are caused} by a single weight."[5]

God the clockmaker

As Carl Sagan has observed, "Kepler stood at a cusp in history; the last scientific astrologer was the first astrophysicist."[6] In his conception of God as a clockmaker, he demonstrates man's extraordinary ability to generalize from what is known, and to draw the conclusions from observations to take us to the next step in our understanding of the way things are. He proposed that the same quantitative physical laws that apply to the Earth are also the quantitative physical laws governing the heavens, and he concluded, "Astronomy is part of physics." Kepler knew the significance of this moment: "With this symphony of voices, man can play through the eternity of time in less than an hour, and can taste in small measure the delight of god, the supreme Artist….I yield freely to the sacred frenzy…the die is cast, and I am writing the book—to be read either now or by posterity, it matters not. It can wait a century for a reader, as God himself has waited 6,000 years for a witness."[7]

Daddy not up there—then where?

The sixteenth-century "climate of opinion" and "race consciousness" did not take kindly to the reduction of God to a mathematician and to the analogy of God's work to making a clock. Kepler was excommunicated from the Lutheran church for his work because it disputed doctrine. His wife and son were wiped out by an epidemic; his mother in his hometown Weil der Stadt in Germany was accused of being a witch, chained and imprisoned in a Protestant dungeon. The witch trials in this single community killed three witches a year between 1615 and 1629. In fact, the dates recall our own Salem, Massachusetts witch trials. This is the great paradox, the great conundrum of human life, that the mind of man can comprehend so clearly, see so perfectly the mathematics of the workings of the Universe, and can be so enmeshed, so mired down in bias, prejudice, hysteria, and cruelty.

From the Cosmos to the Scapegoat

In Kepler's *Somnium*, in addition to imagining man in space travel, he tried to understand himself why he became such a scapegoat. He questioned why his life unfolded as it did, why there was so much religious persecution, why the fear of demons led people to torture his mother and women like her. Kepler's mind soared through the Universe, contemplated the cosmos, met God in Geometry, the clockmaker of planetary motion. Yet his body was trapped amidst the prejudices, fears, horrors, and sorrows of a race consciousness that has accompanied us on our journey since man's very beginning, the mind-set that we pass down generation to generation, that allows to mold and fester the dark side of us, the part that judges and condemns and hurts others. Kepler died outcast, without financial support. The oxen and the eagle, he composed his own epitaph: "I measured the skies, now the shadow I measure. Sky-bound was the mind, Earth-bound the body rests."[8]

Galileo imprisoned for telling truth

The earth-bound persecution for scientific discovery through observation did not end with Kepler. Indeed, it continued. Kepler died in 1630. In 1633 Galileo, the first astronomer to study the movement of the heavens with a telescope, was forced to stand trial by the Catholic hierarchy for "vehement suspicion of heresy." He spent the last eight years of his life under "house arrest" in his home near Florence. In 1615 he had written to the Grand Duchess Christina:

> Some years ago, as Your Serene Highness well knows, I discovered in the heavens many things that had not been seen before our own age. The novelty of these things, as well as some consequences which followed from them in contradiction to the physical notions commonly held among academic philosophers, stirred up against me no small number of professors {many of them ecclesiastics} as if I had placed these things in the sky with my own hands in order to upset Nature and overturn the sciences. They seem to forget that the increase of known truth stimulates the investigation, establishment, and growth of the arts.[9]

Man's unique place in the great chain of being

As we noted earlier in the chapter "Man Is an Astronaut," man holds a unique place in the great chain of being of the universe. The creative mind, force, power, spirit that put this planet into place and action, that which I call God and Fuller calls "Universe," pronounced *it* as done, and *it* was. Whether this came by way of a big bang or by way of Michelangelo's depiction on the ceiling of the Sistine Chapel, the planet is, has been and will continue to be. We as human beings are one stage in evolution of inhabitants here. But we are unique, unique in the place that we hold, for we learn by understanding through trial and error, communicate what we discover, and know by being understood.

Man's know-how

Fuller believes that the lack of an operating manual for the planet is intentional. In that way, we have developed our know-how. Primitive man ate white berries and then red berries and discovered that the red would nourish him and the white would kill him. The nature of the berries does not change. All that changes is our knowledge about the effect of the berries. As we evolved, we learned to cultivate the red berries that would nourish us. We may have even discovered a medicinal use for the white berries. The planets and the heavens did not change in their movement between the writing of Ptolemy, Copernicus, and Kepler. All that changed was our understanding. The operation of the universe and of our planet is purposeful. Our human purpose is to discover what that purpose is and to use it effectively for our collective good. Each of us has a special genius and is a part of that purpose.

Retracing creation of perfect mind

Fuller intellectualizes, systematizes, and mechanizes a frame of reference that goes back to the earliest records of man thinking about himself. Fuller calls the maker of the planet Universe. He conceives of Universe as a perfect mind at work creating a perfectly operable machine. He would be comfortable with

Kepler's co-equivalence of God and Geometry, with the universe as a perfect giant clock; for his work always is based in geometry, on the perfect synchronicity of systems.

Discovery through trial and error

We, the inhabitants of this universe and this planet, are assigned the task, by our very existence here, to figure things out, to discover that perfection of operation. The mechanical lessons in themselves just are. They have no emotion. We learn the mechanical lessons through trial and error. We generalize from what we discover, and we make new applications. We named this process *the scientific method* long after we began to use it. Universe places no limit on this activity, for there is no limit to our thought. The issues are intensified, however, when these mechanical discoveries have generalized application. It affects how we think about our human condition; and it alters how we regard ourselves, how we interact, and how we interface with other people. To place Fuller's frame of reference into the history of man thinking about himself, I am providing "The Metaphysical Context."

The time will come when diligent research over long periods will bring to light things which now lie hidden. A single lifetime, even though entirely devoted to the sky, would not be enough for the investigation of so vast a subject....And so this knowledge will be unfolded only through long successive ages. There will come a time when our descendants will be amazed that we did not know things that are so plain to them....Many discoveries are reserved for ages still to come, when memory of us will have been effaced. Our universe is a sorry little affair unless it has in it something for every age to investigate....Nature does not reveal her mysteries once and for all.

Seneca, Natural Questions, Book VII

Into every intelligence there is a door, which is never closed, through which the creator passes. The intellect, seeker of absolute truth, or the heart, lover of absolute good, intervenes for our succor, and at one whisper of this high power we awake from ineffectual struggles with this nightmare.

Emerson, Experience [1]

The Metaphysical Context

Musty smell of discovery

What first attracted me to Fuller was his optimism, his belief in the absolute ability of the human mind and spirit to figure anything out. It was a consciousness of necessity, a belief that all discoveries are waiting to be made, that the Universal Mind put it all into action and is forever unfolding through us in our evolution. One of his friends from his Black Mountain Days in North Carolina recalls Fuller observing that whenever he made a new discovery, it seemed to have a musty smell, as if it had waited a long time to be opened. Part of this optimism was the belief that everything in our universe works perfectly, has always worked perfectly. The only thing that has changed is our understanding of how it works. Thus, our knowledge grows exponentially, because the more we understand about the physical principles of the function of the universe, the more tools we have to pry open the next secret.

Physical and Metaphysical

Fuller made distinctions that are critical to the application of his ideas: between the physical and the metaphysical, between the brain and the mind. The physical is the observation of the principles of physical universe functioning. For instance, we use the physical principle of leverage to jack up our cars, to create levers and pulleys, to build dams and roads and bridges. In each instance we are doing more with less physical effort. We take the same idea, the same way of doing something, or the same creative act, and we apply it beyond the physical. There is no limit to the metaphysical application. It moves outward in the realm of mind. Exchanges are made, mind to mind, thought to thought, and they are instantaneous. How long does it take to change one's mind? How long does it take to accept a thought? The mind moves in fractions of a second. The metaphysical application moves outward in physical production.

Leverage applied: physical to metaphysical

We use the metaphysical principle of leverage in our monetary system, in our mortgages to buy homes, where the down payment, the lever, lifts up the rest of the cost of the home. We use it when we write a single book and print a million copies, when we record a concert and sell 200,000 CD's, when we produce a single film and make $15 million the first weekend it's distributed, and when we then bring the same movie out as a video, rent and sell it all over the world. There is no limit to how many copies can be made of a single performance of any activity. If we ever doubted that God meant us to live in an abundant universe, we have only to contemplate man's metaphysical application of physical law and physical creation. Universe, this perfect mind that put our perfect universe into existence, is forever giving. God is a great giver. Fuller believes that is the message conveyed by Jesus when he fed the multitude with five loaves and two fishes.

Brain and Mind
The brain

The distinction between brain and mind is also fundamental and definitely a part of the distinction between the physical and metaphysical. We know where the brain is located in the human body. We have surgeons who can go into the brain, who know the neurons and synapses, who can disconnect and re-connect. We have names for parts of the brain: the cortex, the frontal lobe, etc. We know the brain is lodged in the cranium of vertebrates, and every new discovery leaves us more in awe of its complexity. The functions of the brain can be replicated. That is what the computer does. Just as the brain in us acts as a computer, so is the computer a replica of the human brain. The programmer breaks down into steps what the human brain performs automatically.

The mind

It is the mind, however, that conceived of the computer, for in the mind, as Robert Browning's Rabbi Ben Ezra discerns, "A whole I see." In the mind we think comprehensively. The mind *is*. The mind has no specific location. As the neuroscientist Peter Fox observes, "The brain exists in space. But now the mind–the mind operates in time alone."[2] We know it as thought. Thought can come and go. Thought is both conscious and subconscious. We know thought by its action within us, through our awareness, through our perceptions. We can share our thoughts with others. We can't take our thoughts back. We know we can direct them and sort them. We can ignore negative thoughts and focus on positive thoughts.

Transformed by thoughts

We can change our thinking. We can look at events in our life; and through our thinking, we can re-interpret them. In our thoughts we can transform handicaps and deficiencies into challenges; we can regard personal loss and tragedy as opportunity for growth; we can re-construct an image of ourselves, of others, of our experience. There is the story of the pianist who was imprisoned and who practiced the piano every day in his mind. When he got out of prison, he performed a concert flawlessly even though he had not touched an actual piano in seven years.

Fuller: Observing mind

Fuller was an inventor, a scientist, an observer of natural phenomena. He comes from the intellect. He celebrates the mind for comprehensive thinking. He appreciates the mind's ability to apprehend how things work, to unite observations in unforeseen ways, to reveal the workings of the universe, and to generalize from discoveries. He extols the limitless activity of mind, its creativity, its comprehension, its ability to grow out of itself and to make more of itself.

Poets and Prophets: Union of mind with spirit and soul

We recall John Milton's observation in *Paradise Lost*, "The mind is its own place, and of itself can make a heaven of hell, a hell of heaven." ll. 254-55. In the works of poets, the mind, the soul, and the spirit become one, expressed as the power of the Infinite Mind, intellectualized by Fuller as "Universe." Infinite Mind speaks to us through our intuition, through sparks of inspiration; that is, when "spirit" is taken in. The metaphysical poets and the romantic poets, in particular, move us into the spiritual realm of mind.

Metaphysical in perspective

Whenever the word "metaphysical" is used, it creates confusion. The word has connotations that are both ameliorative and pejorative, that are complimentary or insulting, enhancing or condemning. In the last few decades of the twentieth century, metaphysical has become associated with crystals and tarot cards and psychics and religious "cults." We recall, however, from our last chapter on "Trial and Error," that at the beginning of science, that is, man's quest to figure out how things in the universe work, astrology and astronomy were one. Ptolemy, Copernicus, and Kepler made discoveries as astrologers.

Early Christianity a cult

Further, we may recall that the early Christians were a "cult," a group of outcast people hiding in the catacombs of Rome. Early man learned to plant by the "signs of the moon," observed the fertility cycles of the female sex were in synchronicity with the moon, noted that certain stones created energy fields around them when placed in specific proximity to the sun, ascertained one individual could receive a flow of ideas and emotions from another at a subliminal level without articulation in words, a phenomenon we give the name "psychic."

The metaphysical and Jacob's Ladder

Here our purpose is to explore the word "metaphysical" in its ameliorative sense. As we do this we are stretching beyond Fuller's intellectualism into the spiritual insight of the centuries. "Meta" physical means just that, beyond the physical.

The symbol of the ladder to explain what distinguishes man from the rest of life on the planet is a part of our iconography, a visual and verbal symbolism to help us understand who we are. Jacob has a dream about a ladder. At the top of the ladder is God the almighty. Jacob sees angels ascending and descending this ladder, acting as intermediaries between the realm of God and the realm of man. God says to Jacob, "I shall call thee Israel," the "chosen." Jacob becomes the link between the carnal and the spiritual, between the body and the soul, between the human and the divine.

Plato and the metaphysical poets

In the Renaissance, a school of poets labeled "metaphysical" explored this connection, symbolically expressed the mystical ability of man to transcend his body, to become one with the Almighty, the center of the universe. They marveled that man was also the center of the universe. They went back to Plato to contemplate his realm of perfection:

> The One is perfect because it seeks for nothing and possesses nothing, and has need of nothing; and being perfect, it overflows, and thus its superabundance produces an Other... Whenever anything reaches its own perfection, we see that it cannot endure to remain itself, but generates and produces some other thing. Not only beings having the power of choice, but also those which are by nature incapable of choice, and even inanimate things, send forth as much of themselves as they can: thus fire emits heat and snow cold and drugs act upon other things...How then should the Most Perfect Being and the First Good remain shut up in itself, as though it were jealous or impotent—itself the potency of all things?... Something must therefore be begotten of it.

Plato, *Enneads*

Great Chain of Being: man the link

All of nature, all of life, whether animate or inanimate is a spin-off of this perfection, of the "Most Perfect Being" and the "First Good" giving of itself. Each is a link in the Great Chain of Being that descended from the heavens, each entity taking its place on the chain in accordance with its ability to know its original perfection.

Alexander Pope sums it up in his *Essay on Man*:

> Vast chain of being! Which from God began,
> Natures aethereal, human, angel, man,
> Beast, bird, fish, insect, what no eye can see,
> No glass can reach; from Infinite to thee,
> From thee to nothing. I,8,237-41

Cosmic order

Pope continues with the observation that even one link out of place would bring a general dissolution to cosmic order:

> —On superior pow'rs
> Were we to press, inferior might on ours;
> Or in the full creation leave a void,
> Where, one step broken, the great scale's destroy'd
> From Nature's chain whatever link you strike,
> Tenth, or ten thousandth, breaks the chain alike.
> I, 8, 241-47

Hierarchy in our collective unconscious

The idea of this "Great Chain of Being," buried deep within our collective consciousness, may explain our perpetual jockeying for position. Has there ever been a time when man has not thought of himself as either "up" or "down," as either "in" or "out," as either "one" or "alienated," as either "accepted" or "rejected." It is all a part of our consciousness of ourselves, a single "self" struggling to get in place, to find itself in the line, to be on first, to be, if not God, then next to God or at least close to God. God knows how things work because God created them. That is God's job.

Work backward

We self-consciously work backward, figuring out the physical laws that govern how things work. Then we generalize and give those laws an application that goes beyond the physical. We do this by trial and error, through the application of the scientific method. This empowers man to take what he has found, to latch on to the idea, to apply the idea in a variety of ways, and to create, an action of *re-creation* of God's creation. Man thus binds resources to his own endeavors, makes of life more than he found it, becomes more human than he would be if he remained "below," linking the mind of man with the mind that made the universe, the Universal Mind, what Wordsworth called "man's unconquerable mind."

The English Romantic poets: a celebration of mind
Percy Bysshe Shelley

The English Romantic poets are great celebrants of this mind, knowing the more we call upon it, the more the mind is available to us, as our imagination. With the mind we can transcend the human body. It is as Shelley says about the poet in his *Defense of Poetry*:

> For he not only beholds intensely the present as it is, and discovers those laws according to which present things are to be ordered, but he beholds the future in the present, and his thoughts are the germs of the flower and the fruit of latest time....A poet participates in the eternal, the infinite and the one; as far as relates to his conceptions, time and place and number are not.[3]

When the poet communes with the infinite, he observes the laws which order the universe; he sees that in the seed is the flower and the fruit, that all exists in the present moment. The poet making poetry captures this moment of apprehension of how the infinite operates, the visitation of divinity in him.

The poetry: the moment immortalized

> Poetry thus makes immortal all that is best and most beautiful in the world; it arrests the vanishing apparitions which haunt the interlunations of life, and veiling them, or in language or in form, sends them forth among mankind, bearing sweet news of kindred joy to those with whom their sisters abide–abide, because there is no portal of expression from the caverns of the spirit which they inhabit into the universe of things. Poetry redeems from decay the visitations of the divinity in man.[4]

Poets: the unacknowledged legislators of the world

We take, then, from the poet, an understanding for and an appreciation of that which we may pass, day after day, and never notice. Shelley believes that poets are the "unacknowledged legislators of the world" because they have seen perfection and they give it expression for us. We know only what we perceive, and the poet expands our field of perception:

> Poetry turns all things to loveliness; it exalts the beauty of that which is most beautiful, and it adds beauty to that which is more deformed; it marries exultation and horror, grief and pleasure, eternity and change; it subdues to union under its light yoke, all irreconcilable things. It transmutes all that it touches, and every form moving within the radiance of its presence is changed by wondrous sympathy to an incarnation of the spirit which it breathes....All things exist as they are perceived; at least in relation to the percipient (perceiver).[5]

Spirit within the body

The poet combines the disparate into oneness and expresses infinite spirit as it is incarnated into the world. We live in the carnal world, the world of the body. Poetry reminds us of the spirit within that body. Our knowledge of what exists is limited by our perception. The poet makes connections for us, becomes our perceiver, and expands our mind's capacity to know perfection.

William Wordsworth
All mind

For Wordsworth, the mind is all there is. He explores how the mind functions creatively in "The Prelude," expressing as does Shelley the power of the mind to see within the life of things, to see the universe whole and then to express it back in all of its diversity, in what he calls "kindred mutations":

> The power, which all
> Acknowledge when thus moved, which Nature thus
> To bodily sense exhibits, is the express

Resemblance of that glorious faculty
That higher minds bear with them as their own.
Book 14, ll 86-90

Nature: the infinite embodied

Wordsworth looks to nature to express the embodied infinite. This becomes a shield against distortion, against gossip, against bad judgment, against expressions of jealousy. In his "Lines Composed above Tintern Abbey," he comments upon the restorative activity of mind contemplating nature to reveal to us the perfection and harmony that underlie all activity and events:

Knowing that Nature never did betray
The heart that loved her; 'tis her privilege,
Through all the years of this our life, to lead
From joy to joy: for she can so inform
The mind that is within us, so impress
With quietness and beauty, and so feed
With lofty thoughts, that neither evil tongues,
Rash judgments, nor the sneers of selfish men
Nor greetings where no kindness is, nor all
The dreary intercourse of daily life,
Shall e'er prevail against us, or disturb
Our cheerful faith, that all which we behold
Is full of blessings. ll. 122-134

Our inner genius by nature restored

When the mind of man is free from restraint, criticism, fear; when the mind of man is in balance, a recipient of the restorative power of nature, then he can best express his genius. We express our genius when, through comprehensive thinking, our mind links unlike elements, through some intuitive flash, making a connection, thereby discovering, or *re*discovering how the universe works. Emerson, a contemporary of Wordsworth, asserts in "Spiritual Laws" this is man's genius:

> ...the quality that differences him from every other, the susceptibility to the one class of influences, the selection of what is fit for him, the rejection of what is unfit, determines for him the character of the universe. A man is a method, a progressive arrangement; a selection principle, gathering his like to him wherever he goes. He takes only his own out of the multiplicity that sweeps and circles round him.[6]

Genius reflected when the known recreated into the unknown

Wordsworth describes the re-creation of the known into the unknown as "genius" in his "Preface" to the *Lyrical Ballads*:

> Of genius the only proof is, the act of doing well what is worthy to be done, and what was never done before: Of genius, in the fine arts, the only infallible sign is the widening the sphere of human sensibility, for the delight, honour, and benefit of human nature. Genius is the introduction of a new element into the intellectual universe: or, if that be not allowed, it is the application of powers to objects on which they had not before been exercised, or the employment of them in such a manner as to produce effects hitherto unknown.[7]

Birth: memory of perfection

As Wordsworth celebrates "man's inconquerable mind" in "Ode: Intimations of Immortality," he expresses the Platonic belief that before birth we all had complete knowledge of perfection, an ancient idea that before our birth, we experienced all aspects of the universe in its perfect form, generating outward from the One.

Our birth is but a sleep and a forgetting:
The Soul that rises with us, our life's Star,
Hath had elsewhere its setting,
And cometh from afar:
Not in entire forgetfulness
And not in utter nakedness,
But trailing clouds of glory do we come
From God, who is our home:
Heaven lies about us in our infancy!
ll.58-66

At the moment of birth, when the soul descends and meets the body, depending upon how hard it smacks, it recalls a portion of the perfection it knew before birth. To Plato, life on earth is a process of recalling however much as we have the capacity to recall. He made his head of state the Philosopher Ruler because he recalled the most. He believed that the best state is ruled by the most enlightened individual.

Our personal genius

How do we make this specific to us? We observe that in each poetic embrace of the universal, the mind of man intuitively becomes one with something greater than he is. That *greater* is in all of us, speaks to us as our intuition. When Karl Jung studied alchemy, he linked the four elements to four psychological functions: earth sensation, water feeling, air thinking, and fire intuition. That Jung regards intuition as fire reminds us that the mind of Shelley's poet burns as a coal at the moment of divine apprehension. For Jung, when the four psychological functions are in harmony, we experience *individuation*, a state of psychic health and wholeness.[8] This is the desired state. If we ignore what our intuition tells us, if we ignore its direction, we are out of harmony and wholeness, we are untrue to ourselves.

When I ask my students to write an essay about their "inner genius," many will frequently say, "Dr. Windsor, I don't have an inner genius." Yet when I talk with them, when I ask them what they do for pleasure, ask them about awards or medals they may have won, ask them what people compliment them for doing, ask them what comes so easily to them that they consider it trivial, they will usually know it. The flash of insight changes their whole physiology. They laugh; their eyes sparkle; they stand taller. What they hear may not meld with the life they are seeking, the work they are preparing for. Yet this intuitive flash directs them to the work God intended them for, their true vocation, that which they are called to do.

In the Summer 2000 issue of *Parabola*, an issue devoted to riddle and mystery, Christian Wertenbaker tells a story told to him by Robert Brown about Mullah Nasr Eddin. I am going to retell it here:

> Muller Nasrudin was on a journey, and stopped for the night in a town where he did not know anyone. He found an inn and slept comfortably. The next morning on awakening, he discovered to his dismay that he did not know who he was. He thought for a while about his predicament, and then decided to go out into the street to see if anyone might recognize him, and tell him who he was. There were many people in the street, but since he was a stranger in the town, no one recognized him. After wandering around a while, he decided to go into a clothing store. Perhaps someone in there...
>
> The shopkeeper pounced on him. 'Ah, good sir, I have just the suit for you. Here, try this on.' The Mullah complied, and tried on several suits and jackets, none of them being quite satisfactory. After humoring the shopkeeper for some time, he turned to him and said:

'Excuse me, my good man, but did you see me come into your store?'

'Well, yes, of course,' the shopkeeper replied, puzzled.

'Tell me then,' said the Mullah, 'how did you know that it was me?'[9]

This story precedes an exploration of the mystery of the relationship between the inner world and the outer world, how we recall who we are. The purpose of this book is to assist you in bringing the inner and outer together, into harmony, into individuation. This involves opening to our intuition, listening to the voice of the *greater* within us, the God within us seeking to express, recalling the light that may have been dimmed, the voice that may have been muffled, the feelings that may have been ignored. The tools I am now going to introduce to you are meant to bring that harmony between the inner and the outer, between that greatness waiting to be tapped and activated and the rough and tumble world in which we find ourselves.

Our magnificent recollection

"Recall" is at the core of Fuller's account of our human voyage on this planet, the action of mind over matter, the observation and discovery of the physical principles upon which universe operates, and the metaphysical application of those physical principles. The Romantic poets idealize this experience and see evil as a manifestation of a greater perfection. Fuller does not concern himself with theological issues, with good vs. evil. His Universal Genius is a geometrician; his universe works like a clock. He has no illusions, however, about power and its use and abuse by human beings. He urges us to understand the mechanism so that we can break free, through the power of our minds and comprehensive thinking, from control, domination, and manipulation, from the rule of sovereign power and the machinations of the Great Pirates.

Man's purpose in harmony with Universe's underlying perfection

In the great scheme of things, Fuller believes that as we achieve understanding of the operation of the universe, we master the tools required to bring us into harmony with the underlying perfection of Universe's operation and the Mind responsible for its creation. With this clarification of physical/metaphysical–mind/brain distinction, we are now ready to explore Fuller's concepts, derived from observing how the planet works. As we do so, we will assume the "idea" that a perfect pattern underlies our experience. If it is muddled or misdirected, we have only to get clear and in touch, through our intuition and through our intellect, with that underlying perfection. Our inner genius will guide us. The steps required to progress to the desired state will then be manifest.

Bill Clinton was playing golf with the
Duke of York on Martha's Vineyard during his vacation. They were sitting in the
golf cart, watching it rain.
The Duke said, "I'll play you for the
island. It used to be ours."
Clinton replied, "Thank God it's raining!"

Earth
"A planet doesn't explode of itself," said drily
The Martian astronomer, gazing off into the air—
"That they were able to do it is proof that highly
Intelligent beings must have been living there."

John Hall Wheelock, 1961

A noiseless patient spider,
I mark'd where on a little promontory it stood isolated,
Mark'd how to explore the vacant vast surrounding
It launch'd forth filament, filament, filament, out of itself,
Ever unreeling them, ever tirelessly speeding them.

And you O my soul where you stand,
Surrounded, detached in measureless oceans of space,
Ceaselessly musing, venturing, throwing, seeking the spheres to
Connect them,
Till the bridge you will need be form'd, till the ductile anchor hold,
Till the gossamer thread you fling catch somewhere, O my soul.

Walt Whitman, 1862-63

The Red Wheelbarrow
so much depends
upon

a red wheel
barrow

glazed with rain
water

beside the white
chickens
William Carlos Williams 1923

Part 3: Tool Kit Of Concepts

* Our planet was run, and still is, by "great pirates" who seize sovereignty over others.

* We can have sovereignty over ourselves, can rule our own lives, by letting go of temporary solutions that no longer serve us and by employing principles and concepts generalized from the perfect operation of the planet.

* We can use our true wealth, our ability to create, plan, and direct the forward days of our life, to create abundance and self-satisfaction.

What we call real estate—the solid ground to build a house on—is the broad foundation on which nearly all the guilt of the world rests....The author has provided himself with a moral—the truth, namely, that the wrongdoing of one generation lives into the successive ones, and divesting itself of every temporary advantage, becomes a pure and uncontrollable mischief; and he would feel it a singular gratification if this romance might effectually convince mankind—or indeed, any one man—of the folly of tumbling down an avalanche of ill-gotten gold, or real estate on the heads of an unfortunate posterity, thereby to maim and crush them, until the accumulated mass shall be scattered abroad in its original atoms.

Nathaniel Hawthorne, *The House of Seven Gables*[1]

Now since the prince must make use of the characteristics of beasts he should choose those of the fox and the lion, though the lion cannot defend himself against snares and the fox is helpless against wolves. One must be a fox in avoiding traps and a lion in frightening wolves. Such as choose simply the role of a lion do not rightly understand the matter. Hence a wise leader cannot and should not keep his word when keeping it is not to his advantage or when the reasons that made him give it are no longer valid. If men were good, this would not be a good precept, but since they are wicked and will not keep faith with you, you are not bound to keep faith with them. We must be like the lion and the fox. Separate Machiavelli, *The Prince* from the text to be consistent with Nathaniel Hawthorne, *The House of Seven Gables*

The Great Pirates

Commodities discovered and distributed

As a real estate broker, I should probably take offense at Hawthorne's observation that "all the guilt of the world rests" on real estate; and yet as an enlightened citizen and student of history, I know that this perfect little planet has been carved up and passed out over the centuries by individuals who have wielded their power and manipulation over others, who have played the lion and the fox. Fuller called these people the Great Pirates, or GP's, and he conceived of the first ones as adventurers with courage and curiosity. They moved from their island of birth by canoe to explore the next island where they discovered commodities unknown at home. This was the origin of trade. At first it might have been as simple as a banana island, a coconut island, a pineapple island, a mango island, and a basket island. The Great Pirate knew where to find each fruit and where to find the basket to hold it.

Beginning of sovereign power

As the Great Pirates accumulated knowledge about the location of different commodities, they also established power for themselves. They were the only ones who knew where everything was. As the task of handling the whole enterprise on their own became too overwhelming, they installed token kings to oversee each distribution center, endowing them with the visual and exterior accoutrements of power: crown, scepter, robe, and elegant hut. They were the sovereign power, i.e. the reigning power over the territory assigned to them by the Great Pirate.

Kings: control by specialization

The kings each knew the functioning of his own island, but knew nothing about the other islands or about exactly what the GP did. Each king was instructed to assign specific jobs on the island. The best mathematician was made treasurer, the best memorizer the secretary, the best organizer the manager of operations. No one was to know anyone else's job, only his own. The only other person, other than the king, who could know every job description was the king's son. In that way knowledge, which is power, was localized in the ruling family. Fuller believes this was the "origin of specialization," a method to keep each individual narrow in scope and limited.

Carving up the planet

As the kingdoms of the kings became more powerful, the kings began exploration on their own, or so it appeared. Always, however, they acted with the GP's guidance, knowledge, and supervision. The GP's preferred to work in the background, anonymously calling the shots and controlling the resources. The kings then marched on continents, on North America, announcing one part to the King of Spain, another part to the King of England. They were represented by people such as Christopher Columbus who didn't know where he was going, and didn't know where he was when he got there. That's why we have Indians in the Americas; because the poor, confused chap thought he was in India. The kings marched on Africa, claiming one territory for the King of Belgium, another for the King of the Netherlands, another for the King of England, and so on. Always the envoy of the king planted a flag and claimed sovereign power, that is, ruling power. The indigenous people let them do it, often without a fight. They may have had law-givers in their tribes, but they had no lawyers.

The beginning of real estate

This was the beginning of real estate, the planet-wide determiner of true wealth because we can measure it, we can't move it, but we can transfer it once we take title to it. Even the word "title" takes us back to the "sovereign" roots of real estate. The original inhabitants, we call them indigenous, at least in the United States, believed that Mother Earth belonged to everyone and had neither the concept nor the vocabulary for such a seizure. Thus our planet was carved up and claimed by kings who reigned sovereign over their territory. The history of man at war is the history of man laying claim to real estate, more often than not in the name of Jehovah, or Allah, or God. In the great war, the Second World War, both sides of the European front declared God as their champion.

Spanish Land Grants

The Spanish explorers came to the Americas: Cortez, Ponce de Leon, Balboa; and everywhere they went, they laid claim for the King of Spain. Is there anything more ridiculous than the historical "facts" we were taught in school, that Ponce de Leon discovered Florida, and Balboa discovered the Pacific Ocean? Southern California was parceled out in Spanish Land Grants from the King of Spain. Real estate empires were formed. The city of Irvine, California, now boasting the highest valued property in Orange County, is built on a Spanish

Land Grant said to have been won by a member of the Irvine family in a poker game. Although the story may be apocryphal, one may well ask how such a story could even be bandied about. Truly, the aggressive, assumptive seizure of property from inhabitants too ignorant and naïve to realize what was happening actually took place. Once they were dispossessed and displaced, they had no power. The Catholic priests tried to deal with kindness. Father Junipero Serra traveled the coast of California founding missions: San Diego, San Juan Capistrano, Santa Monica, Santa Barbara, San Jose, Santa Cruz, San Francisco, to name only a few. The priests in the missions then worked with the indigenous people, teaching them what they knew.

Indian Reservations
Sites with worthless real estate

As we consider the history of the North American Indians, we know that the early pilgrim settlers would have had great difficulty surviving without their help. Yet just as the pilgrims entered a land controlled by a distant king, so also did that king claim control of the indigenous residents. When the newcomers declared independence and wrested power from the king, the new government assumed sovereignty over those who first welcomed them. The Indians were pushed and pulled by the wars of the invaders. In the French and Indian War, most Indians fought with the French against the British; yet the Senecas fought with the British. As the U.S. government expanded into new territories, the Indian lands were seized, and their people were sent off to reservations. The land was carefully selected as the worst real estate in the United States.

Sovereign power exempt from rights of U.S. citizens

Ironically, under that real estate, the tribes have sometimes found natural resources, making them wealthy. The Cherokees, for instance, moved by forced walk on the Trail of Tears to their Oklahoma reservation, became wealthy from the oil under their land. A further irony, the Indians were given sovereign power over their territory, independent from the U.S. government. Although this was designed to deny them the benefits of American citizenship, it means also that their territory is independent from U.S. laws and restrictions. As the Indians have educated themselves in the ways of power, their own Harvard graduate GP's have emerged; and they have turned this to their advantage, with banks, casinos, and bingos, immune to lawsuits, exempt from most taxes, and excluded from labor laws. Now the government regards this as an "area of concern" because it "wasn't what was meant" when the Indians were first segregated from the rights, privileges, and opportunities of living in America, their original home, but their denied nation.

Great Pirates always in the background
Joseph Kennedy: a great pirate

Great Pirates do not run for office, do not expose themselves to the public, do not divulge their *modus operandi*. They work through other people. As the sovereign nations have matured and granted voting rights to their people, elected officials have replaced the kings, but still with the backing and control of the Great Pirates. It has reached ridiculous proportions as we enter the new millennium when election predictions are based, not upon the qualifications, but upon the fund raising capacity of the candidates.

The curse of the Great Pirate

Our twentieth century in the United States is absorbed with the story of the Kennedy family: So much charm, so much dedication to public service, so much potential, so much money, yet so much tragedy. After the death in a plane crash of John Kennedy Jr., the only son of John F. Kennedy and Jacqueline Bouvier Kennedy, the media began to talk about a curse on the family, a curse from the ill-got fortune of the father, Joseph Kennedy, a great pirate who acquired his wealth as a rum-runner, trading in liquor during prohibition when it was illegal. They were asking, was it this origin in evil that led to the chain of tragedy: the early death of the first-born son, Joseph, in World War II; the assassinations of John F. Kennedy when he was President, and of Bobby Kennedy, when he was running for president; the early death of Kathleen; the murky circumstances surrounding the drowning of Ted Kennedy's companion and his flight from the scene of the accident?

A dynasty of kings

Curse or no curse, it is an emblematic case of the great pirate and the king, or rather, President, in our American democracy. Although he served one brief appointment as Ambassador to Great Britain, Joseph Kennedy could never have run for office. His fortune was not appropriately acquired, and he would have been too rough-hewn to be elected. He worked as a Great Pirate, gaining social stature and respectability by marrying into the Fitzgerald family, an old Boston family with pedigree. He had twelve children by his wife, Rose; and of those twelve, three sons rose to high positions in the U.S. government, as senators and then one as president, John Fitzgerald Kennedy. There is no doubt the legacy of public service will continue into this next century through the grandchildren. Already Patrick, son of Robert, is making a name for himself in the senate and others are expected to run for office. Joseph Kennedy was behind the scenes during his son's campaign for President, directing and controlling the activities and the flow of money. He was a master at manipulating public opinion. When the book, *Profiles in Courage*, was published, it is said that he bought up all of the copies and warehoused them, thus making his son's book a best seller overnight.

The hierarchy of having

Other than cynical awareness, what good does it do to look at the history of the world as the manipulation of GPs? It can place in perspective where we feel we are in the "hierarchy of having." If it is true that seven "moneyed" families control the financial world of the planet, then life appears pretty much to be divided: The *haves* and the *have-nots*; the *ins* and the *outs*; the *givers* and the *takers*; the *shapers* and *recipients*; the *powerful* and the *powerless*; the *controllers* and the *controlled*. Those who *have*, who are *in*, who *give*, and who *shape* know abundance, self-confidence, and presumably peace and harmony. Those who *have-not*, who are *out*, who *take* what's handed to them and who *receive* policy, who are *powerless*, live in scarcity, insecurity, and envy.

Kings as executioners

Fuller believes that specialization began when the Great Pirates appointed kings and told them to assign jobs to their constituents, but to not let anyone do or know anyone else's job. If anyone else knew what he and his son knew, then he could be king. In fact, the fascinating thing about being on the high side—*Have, In, Give, Shape, Power, Control*—is that as soon as you're there, you worry about staying there, about protecting what you have and know, about keeping the other side in its place. The word *execute* means to carry out. Yet note how the connotation of *execution* comes first into our minds as an act of violence, of seizing life from another. It also applies to seizing *life work* from another.

The history of the kings of England provides a perfect example. As soon as a man became king, usually by executing the king before him, he was uneasy about staying king, began to execute potential opponents, and ultimately was executed himself by the next king. Probably most of us know Shakespeare's play, *Macbeth*, as well as any. As you may recall from the play, the moment Macbeth has murdered to become king, "Macbeth has murdered sleep." It begins his path of *paranoia,* until both he and Lady Macbeth, overcome by guilt and anxiety, lose their ability to function effectively. They madly begin to destroy any potential contenders to the throne, the competition. Yet, ultimately they are defeated when the "woods come to Dunsinane," the prediction of the three witches. They are attacked by soldiers who march on them with trees tied to their helmets, a veritable moving woods.

Competitive seizure and elimination

You don't have to be king of anything to know the fear of protecting a position once you've got the job. This is what we learn from the Great Pirates: how to seize and how to keep control. Bill Gates surrounds himself with the brightest and the best at Microsoft because he comes from a place of self-confidence and self-satisfaction. As one moves away from his attitude, at the other end of the spectrum, we have large institutions, especially bureaucratic ones, that operate as formalized GP's, with boxes, boundaries, and rules for each position.

Each working individual exists in a situation somewhere between the two extremes. People in established positions often feel driven to box in and put down others who might either pose as threats or make them look inadequate. Have you ever been told you are not to overstep your bounds? When you are at the bottom in the "hierarchy of having," you belong to the "company store." You have no sovereignty over your destiny. An aggressive, ambitious, bright young person may be labeled "arrogant," and the word may go out: "Watch out for him. He's ambitious."

Programmatic elimination

Since the early part of my life experience took place at the bureaucratic extreme, in *academia*, many opportunities arose for me to encounter reaction by those in power to people who were an apparent threat to them. For instance, I once served on a search committee for an open position within a University's Humanities department. The wife of a Professor, a fine Renaissance scholar trained at Yale, was eliminated from the finalists although she had better credentials than the person hired. She also had better credentials than most of the Humanities faculty represented on the search committee. In fact, the search committee was composed predominately of women who had experienced doors slammed for them because of nepotism. Where one might have anticipated compassion for the predicament of this highly trained, unemployed wife with talents and gifts to share, rather they chose "to do unto her as they had been done to" by eliminating her under the pretense her specialty was "too narrow." They made a programmatic decision rather than a human decision. To prove, however, that adversity always moves us to a better place, this woman was eventually called back to Yale and joined its faculty, and her husband went to teach at the nearby State University in Connecticut.

Self-realization: self-employment

The university is an extreme; yet any decision to eliminate because of downsizing is a programmatic decision, and it can happen to anyone who has no control over his destiny. In a bureaucratic institution, a kluge operation, one is the recipient of a system designed by GP's long gone who left in place unquestioned process and procedure. Old rules form the basis of decision-making, and people in power positions use them for self-protection. If this book has one underlying message, it would be that self-realization can best be achieved through self-employment. Self-employment exists in thought and is a state of mind. When you hold yourself as the president of your own company, interfacing with clients and colleagues, you retain your integrity, and you retain sovereignty over your activities. You are a great pirate in your life, determining the flow of activity, the course of your path.

The pinnacle and the base

Emerson says, "the pinnacle cannot exceed the base." In my own career in *academia*, which stretched over two decades, the base stood, but the system resisted the pinnacle. I am using myself as an example of one for whom self-realization and self-employment are inextricably linked, something I didn't know until I found myself in the role of an administrator in a bureaucracy. This is a story about hitting a wall and then being challenged to figure out the appropriate environment to use my abilities. Each of us faces this challenge and will not know satisfaction until we have achieved this understanding.

As a "high achiever," I had put myself through all my degrees, finished a doctoral degree, taken a job at a small women's college as an assistant professor, been promoted to chairman of the department, assumed leadership in every one of the major committees in the college, written a few articles published in acceptable journals, taught classes from the beginning to the present in English literature, and developed a following of students and faculty. This is what an academician is supposed to do. When the financial problems at that small college became so severe that it began to consume my life, and when the leadership of the college fell in a way that made me uncomfortable, I accepted an administrative position at a University directing an academic program in a residence hall. It required that I give up the tenure granted at the end of my third year at my former institution. It didn't occur to me to worry about it since I had been continuously employed since the age of thirteen.

Accidental achievement ok

Once again, a pattern of success emerged, easily and effortlessly, just as Emerson's little bark makes its way to sea. My vision expanded to the creation of another academic program in a second residence hall, based upon the model of Yale's residential colleges and the University of Michigan's residential college. This would give the students a focus for creative living in an energized academic environment. It was the late '70s. The University was a party school. The students were consumed with alcohol and drugs and in the morning, the halls would be littered with bottles and cans from the partying the night before. In my 8:00 a.m. class in Humanities, my students would sit bleary-eyed through my sales pitch for Aeschylus, Plato, Sophocles, Euripides, and Homer.

Drive and ambition not ok

As my passion to change and improve this situation grew into a plan with specific goals, others followed and supported me. In fact, we moved the second residential program through every necessary committee with record speed, all the way up the Chancellor for final approval. Up to that time, my accomplishments were made with my left hand, putting my family before a career and without taking myself seriously. As my efforts began to reflect greater earnestness and zeal, however, forces simultaneously began to align against me. Drive and ambition are acceptable in entrepreneurs, but not in bureaucrats.

Lowest common denominator

In every bureaucratic institution, the lowest common denominator ultimately dominates. Whenever an individual even appears to be rocking that lowest common denominator, the power structure rallies to obliterate it. The system does not tolerate innovation. Protection of the *status quo* informs and shapes the process of decision-making. Since I had been working so hard all my life, keeping my "nose to the grindstone," this understanding of my surroundings was never clear to me, the big picture of how the power structure actually functions. On the one hand, in retrospect, the university represented for me the safe haven of the insecure academic. Yet, on the other hand, in my heart I was a self-made entrepreneur, and consequently for *academia*, "a duck out of water."

The work obsession

All my life I knew nothing but work. It was taught in my home. Work, the idea of work, so Puritanical, so Germanic, narrowly defined existence for me. Emerson says, "Do your work and I shall know you." It was not that kind of work, not the *calling*. It was work, the being busy, each mediocre accomplishment a means for a definition of self. We all deal with adolescence as best we can. Since I was not a Barbie doll with perfect body, perfect hair, and perfect clothes, I forged my identity through work and became a perfect taskmaster: working for my parents in their business at the golf course, chairing the clarinet section in the band and orchestra up to the state level, and maintaining a high enough grade-point average to be valedictorian of my class, fulfilling my mother's intention. Although I received several scholarships for the University of Michigan, my day-to-day survival required taking every part-time job that turned up: book store, baby sitting, assisting at weekly teas at the International Center and the President's home. My political science teacher once commented that he went to three teas in one week and observed me working at each of them. I worked every summer at the golf course until I graduated, and then I worked half time at the School of Public Health to complete my master's degree in two semesters. From there I went immediately into marriage and on to more work.

Totally insecure

In the course of this activity, I never had a room of my own. During my childhood, someone was always living with us: aunts, uncles, cousins, then my sisters. There was never quite enough room, and my needs and wants were subordinate to circumstances. In fact, in my mind subordination was the appropriate state and self-assertion the inappropriate state. This was true with my teachers, my parents, and then my husband. The outer self-assurance, confidence, effectiveness enclosed the inner assumption of unworthiness. The choice of Virginia Woolf, the author of *A Room of One's Own*, as the subject for my doctoral dissertation, was surely an Emersonian act of "compensation."

The safe haven

Academia was the perfect place for someone with my issues so long as I didn't take myself seriously or question subordination. My complexes remained hidden even to me because I just kept working. When that work became a mission and a form of self-definition, however, when it became really important to me, it was taken away. The head of housing considered me both a nuisance and a threat because he was afraid I would go through the University and put an academic program in every residence hall. He was right; that was my intent. In the meantime, that same group of humanists, built into this newly created program as the cornerstone, ganged up against me behind my back.

Be paranoid

My focus on activity and results and my basic naivety blinded me to the machinations occurring around me. Where was Donald Trump then? Be paranoid! Get even! When I left, they replaced me with a male triumvirate, and then the humanities department moved in and took over. So many power plays over such a piddling pond!

I was surrounded by people just like me, filled with self-importance.

Hassling the hierarchy

This experience highlighted some of the more challenging aspects of my personality, especially impatience and "envisioning zeal." My husband at the time would shrink fearfully away from my tendency to view reality from my imagination, i.e., the way it would be when I had molded it to my vision. His concern was what it would take from him to get to my envisioned reality. The greater my exuberance, the more he would feel threatened. My operation with the university was similar: going over and around people, not "observing the hierarchy," moving as a bulldozer. That's exactly what an entrepreneur does. So long as I was in the classroom, the entrepreneurial side manifested in creative ways to present the material to the students. I actually lacked the basic constitution to be an administrator, and I still do. Academic administrators spend their entire days in meetings where little is accomplished. My favorite analogy is taking a male dog for a walk. Each person present pees on the tree, gets his name in the minutes, and the job is complete. The tree is watered, the day is over, major issues are tabled, and the next meeting is set. It drove me crazy.

The scorpion

Huxley talks about how the scorpion, when it is surrounded, stings everything in sight. My reaction involved a fair share of stinging, especially after getting stung. When a graduate student in Women's Studies interviewed me to learn how I managed to break through the bureaucracy, the apparent pinnacle, I observed that my appointment was non-tenure, administrative, and subject to removal with two week's notice. I self-predicted the closure. Actually, they gave me a year of teaching at full administrative pay, the penance of a Dean, and during that year I began my transition into business.

Create and move on

Although the Dean of the law school and head of the local ACLU urged me to sue and offered to represent me *pro bono*, I declined. When other women similarly assaulted by the system undertook such law suites, they directed attention so obsessively into the past that there was no living in the present or projection into a productive future. My final choice: create and move on. Actually, that fits the pattern of an entrepreneur. As a paradigm for my first change of career, I hold a remark made to me at a party by the wife of a Dean: "Well, now you finally have a job to match your wardrobe."

Thankful for faults

A part of me is still the person who had this experience, but I am impatient with her now. She irritates me because her egotistical perspective blew the puny little plot of land she was tilling into such importance. The program actually still continues. Several years later, when my son was an undergraduate at Harvard, he directed one of the Harvard Student Agencies and hired a summer school student from the University. The student said, "I'm in this great two-year academic program. It's the best thing the University has." My son said, "Yes, I know about that program. My mother created it." Institutions, says Emerson, are the "lengthened shadow" of the individual. The individual is long gone, and the institution assumes a vitality of its own.

Worthy of compassion

This woman, the one that makes me impatient, also has my compassion. I was shattered for three reasons: 1) I defined myself by work, and my work was taken away. 2) I prided myself on successful achievement, and I was punished for success. 3) I assumed that all of my life I would work for someone else, and that if I played the game properly, I would have a solid career. My identity belonged to the structure, to the system, to the hierarchy, rather than to myself. My life was outer directed and determined, not inner directed and determined. To be punished for success turned everything I had worked for upside down. I was disoriented.

Inevitable calamity

This was the beginning of a path of life from the inside out rather than from the outside in. It was one of those Emersonian-defined moments when I was forced to shed the house I had outgrown, and it required a calamity to jolt me on to the next step. Certainly, I would do many things differently now, because my central focus is grounded in a more spiritual place. Today the obstacles would present themselves as challenges placed in my path for a purpose. Since my life path has led me into mediation training, there would be more listening and less talking. Emerson's observation that "every man in his lifetime needs to thank his faults" sums up this experience. Being who I was at the time, brought about a turn in the road that led me down a far different path, one probably more suited to my temperament and certainly more tolerant of change and zeal.

New navigation tools.

I was forced to become a "great pirate." My departure from *academia* led me to develop aspects of myself I didn't know existed. Because the University of Michigan believed that philosophy and mathematics were co-equivalent in perfecting logical thinking, I avoided math. Similarly, I backed away from economics because it was reputed to be too hard and a bad grade might jeopardize my scholarships. For myriad wrong reasons, I limited my experience of a way of thinking and an approach to interpreting reality for which I had a definite aptitude.

The first major new direction in my life, training as a stockbroker, made me a salmon swimming up-stream. My class was full of people who were MBA's in finance, real estate brokers, CPA's. From the shelter of the university, I didn't have a clue how the real world worked. When we bought our first house, we didn't understand anything about either the contract or the closing statement except the monthly mortgage payment. We just assumed the realtor and the bank were trustworthy. Yet with all of this apparent limitation, I had within me the ability to master this new field, to pass the Series 7, and then later to master financial analysis of commercial real estate for acquisition.

A matter of zeroes

The sales training as a stock broker centered on cold calling. They started us out qualifying buyers for municipal bonds. We had a list of people to call, and our first statement would be, "This requires a minimum investment of $5000. Would that be a problem for you?" I literally choked, actually croaked, over that statement for at least the first fifty calls. As an academic I had never dreamed about spending that much money on something to put away in a safe deposit box. Over the course of my career I have come to realize it is just a matter of more zeroes to go from $5,000 to $50,000,000. The people are pretty much the same. It is just a different product.

More zeroes, same quirks

Once I became accustomed to zeroes, I got carried away by them for a while. During the frantic period when the Japanese were buying out American commercial real estate, I participated in a team that put an office complex for $250,000,000 into escrow. The deal didn't close because the buyers at the end were not able to come up with the funds, but the adrenalin rush was great. I also wore myself out for several years trying to sell 1100 acres of raw land in Malibu with ocean frontage. The owner, who once had owned two miles along the coast of the Pacific Ocean, wanted $80,000,000 cash, a big chunk for a property not permitted by the Coastal Commission. He loved to show the property to buyers, to buy them a lobster and clam chowder lunch at his favorite restaurant, to make it a glorious day-outing, but I finally realized he didn't want to let go of the property. On weekends he would take his little lawn chair out to the property and just sit there.

Although I brought him several capable buyers, he never would accept their offers. I finally gave up when I took him an offer for $20,000,000 cash and $564,000 a month for the next twenty years. He made a classic comment: "Adrian, you know I can't live on $564,000 a month." The other broker called me the next day and said, "I don't understand how he can smile while he is making such obnoxious statements." I explained that he was on his third face lift, and the last one left him with a constant, stretched smile.

Just like you and me

In business and in life today, I carry as a touchstone a conversation that I once had with Ann Love, the wife of Governor John Love of Colorado. As a young assistant professor, only twenty-seven, I was the faculty's elected representative to a search committee for a new president of the college. The committee was chaired by Walt Kobel, the developer of Vail, Colorado, and the members of the committee were well-recognized state leaders, to me absolutely awesome. The candidates who came for interviews were equally eminent, and I was impressed by the way Ann Love always put them at their ease, always knew exactly what to say and when to say it. When I finally knew her well enough to ask her about it, she said, "I just remember that they are just like you and me. They get hungry; they have to go the bathroom; they need to call home to their families." As the zeroes in the numbers have increased in the products I deal with, I remember her words. The consumers, the people buying, are just like you and me. The sellers have the same anxieties, neuroses, and quirks.

Mastery

Each time I have changed career, I have mastered a new vocabulary. That is the bottom line. The infinitive "to master" is critical. That is what the Great Pirates did, and that is what they continue to do. They create sovereignty, control, through mastery. The Great Pirate techniques stood me in good stead. Because I knew how to read for comprehension, how to master the new vocabulary, how to discern what was crucial from what was tangential, how to prepare for an examination, and how to predict what would be stressed as essential knowledge, I was able to master a new specialization. Now that I have done it several times, each time it gets easier, perhaps because having done it once, the assurance is there to do it again. The adrenalin charge of the challenge has replaced the anxiety. Both are stimulants to the body, but one moves you forward, and the other stops you in your tracks. Charge up and move forward.

Transfer of skills

Further, all of the skills as a teacher, a counselor, and an administrator have been essential in each undertaking. Because both financial services and real estate understanding came to me as an adult learner, I can intuitively uncover areas of confusion in my clients and can clarify issues simply and directly. With a contract, I often teach the contract as I write it so nothing is left unstated or obfuscated. Further, since most decisions we make in life initiate first from emotion and second by reason, my intuitive powers and my listening skills are more important than any amount of book learning.

Out of control

The issue of control, of keeping someone "in his place" because he may be a threat, is very common in the workplace. My example is extreme because *academia* is so bureaucratized and the players are so boxed in by the system. Yet, similar situations arise in any institution. If you're too good at what you do, your boss is afraid you will get her job. If you have total enthusiasm for your work, and you find yourself among others who have grown stale and dreary, the light of your star will be drenched lest it illuminate the dullness evoked by your competitors. Do not believe that you are a victim of these circumstances. Rather, know and accept that you have been challenged by them so that you may discover within yourself the resources for greater growth. Let your light shine, if not where you are, then somewhere else. It will be better for you and better for everyone else. Be out of control.

Beyond definition

Further, we live in a society where technological expertise is so critical we are forced to specialize in order to get hired. In his book, *The End of Work*, Jeremy Rifkin predicts that by approximately 2020 there will be no blue collar jobs in the manufacturing sector and that even the majority of our service jobs will be replaced by automation. A protest against World Trade will not stop the momentum. The change seems to be coming faster than 2020. Some banks charge clients $2 each time they have the audacity to come in and use the teller in the lobby rather than the ATM machine. Yet the truth of technology is that it changes so fast, one's specialty is constantly in jeopardy of being eliminated. We need to know that we can master any new field, that we are not limited by external forces. Nothing exists in the universe except thought and energy. When you think of yourself as self-employed, it changes your orientation toward your employment. Be an independent contractor in your mind.

Knowledge the key

The key to moving from the vulnerable low side—*Have-Nots, Outsiders, Takers, Recipients, Powerless, Controlled*—to the high side—*Haves, Ins, Givers, Shapers, Empowered, In Control*—is knowledge. It is increasingly impossible today for those who have knowledge to keep it to themselves because we have access from so many sources opened by the computer and the Internet. We all have the ability to learn everyone else's job, i.e. to move out of the specialization that keeps us in a narrow niche, vulnerable to downsizing and elimination. If we master the tools of comprehensive thinking, we can master any field at any time.

No limits

We are not limited by birth or station from access to knowledge. We can become educated at home, at community colleges, by distance learning. We have no set timetable. Education and learning are life-long. We do not need stock-brokers to become investors. We can trade over the Internet. The commodity market isn't just for Great Pirates. A small group of Japanese college students, for instance, got together when the yen fell in value. They pooled their student loans and bought yen. When their investment doubled, they sold.

Your tools

The tools and concepts presented here will prove useful in gaining confidence, in thinking comprehensively, and in establishing sovereignty over your life. The purpose of this book is to help you get your mind-set on the high side, to assist you in your move from scarcity to abundance, from vulnerability to empowerment. As we realize that we can now all be Great Pirates within our realm, the control of the ostensible Great Pirate diminishes, loses its dominance.

Blessed past

The following exercise will give you an opportunity to consider skills you have that are transferable, i.e. what you had to master to do what you do or what you did. Also, take a little time to let go of "bad" things that might have happened to you in the workplace. I just did. As Emerson points out to us in his essay "Compensation," adversity forces us to leave behind old associations, old patterns of behavior, old ways of approaching problems. It brings out our resilience, our survival instinct; and it taps abilities we never knew we had:

> A fever, a mutilation, a cruel disappointment, a loss of wealth, a loss of friends, seems at the moment unpaid loss, and unpayable. But, the sure years reveal the deep remedial force that underlies all facts. The death of a dear friend, wife, brother, lover, which seemed nothing but privation, somewhat later assumes the aspect of a guide or genius; for it commonly operates revolutions in our way of life, terminates an epoch of infancy or of youth which was waiting to be closed, breaks up a wonted occupation, or a household, or style of living, and allows the formation of new ones more friendly to the growth of character.[3]

In the process we leave behind the house we have outgrown, and we are ready to build a new house. You may be ready to close the garage door and to come out on the front porch.

BECOMING A GREAT PIRATE

LIFETIME OCCUPATIONS:

List the worst job experiences you have ever had. Return to the emotions you have about those jobs. What was happening? What did the people look like? Put yourself back into the memory.

Fuller believes that *"society operates on the theory that specialization is the key to success, not realizing that specialization precludes comprehensive thinking."* For each occupation listed above, state the specialized skill it required and the comprehensive knowledge you acquired in achieving that specialized skill. Comprehensive knowledge may include such things as following a procedure; mastering a vocabulary; establishing a timetable for completing tasks or fulfilling a discipline, for instance making 20 phone calls a day, etc.

JOB	SPECIALIZED SKILL	COMPREHENSIVE KNOWLEDGE

How can you become a Great Pirate in your life?
List areas in your life where you can be in control through comprehensive knowledge.

_____

_____

_____

_____

_____

_____

_____

The thought of being in control, of taking control makes me feel...

_____

_____

_____

_____

_____

_____

_____

In the past, I have preferred to be controlled by others in these situა

_____

_____

_____

_____

_____

_____

_____

_____

_____

_____

In reviewing these situations, I conclude this about their service to good:

_____

_____

_____

_____

_____

_____

_____

_____

_____

_____

_____

_____

The changes which break up at short intervals the prosperity of men are advertisements of a nature whose law is growth. Every soul is by this intrinsic necessity quitting its whole system of things, its friends and home and laws and faith, as the shell-fish crawls out of its beautiful but stony case, because it no longer admits of its growth, and slowly forms a new house.

Emerson, Compensation [1]

Piano Tops

Temporary life-savers

R. Buckminster Fuller opens *Operating Manual for Spaceship Earth* with this statement: "If you are in a shipwreck and all the boats are gone, a piano top buoyant enough to keep you afloat that comes along makes a fortuitous life preserver. This is not to say that the best way to design a life preserver is in the form of a piano top. I think that we are clinging to a great many piano tops in accepting yesterday's fortuitous contrivings as constituting the only means for solving a given problem."[2] It's much easier to visualize the top of a grand piano floating by, acting as a temporary life saver, since the release and tremendous popularity of *Titanic*. And although a piano top may not be the best way to make a lifesaver, here at the beginning of the twenty-first century, alas, we observe humanity clinging to a great many piano tops that were meant to be temporary solutions; and, indeed, in many cases we have come close to institutionalizing the piano top. As a nation we see it in our defense, in our education, in our government. We also see it in our personal lives, in our relationships, in our jobs, in our methods of confronting challenges.

Planetary disarmament a distant dream

Fuller believed the future of humanity would rest upon planetary disarmament, hoping that weapons of destruction to claim sovereignty or to protect sovereignty would no longer be needed by the end of the century. Yet, now, after the century has turned, we recognize that world peace has not come, that the best deterrent to war is still preparation for war. Instead of nuclear weapons in the hands of two nations, now they are spread out among both the developed and the undeveloped. The nations are too unpredictable.

India tested a nuclear weapon; then Pakistan tested one, too, in protest. Then Pakistan's government was seized by the military. The President of the United States overrode Congress and allowed an American company to sell China a missile delivery system. Then we discovered that a Chinese scientist working at Los Alamos tapped into U.S. nuclear secrets. China has aimed its planes and helicopters defiantly at Taiwan, so Taiwan has aimed its planes and helicopters at China. Does the U.S. truly have a one-China policy, or if Taiwan were attacked, would the U.S. defend the island? We don't even want to know. Russia, not invited into NATO, insisted on being part of a peacekeeping force in Kosovo. *60 Minutes* reported on a Russian facility that continues the nuclear build-up. Russian military planes flew over Greenland. The U.S. sent them back. Russia said they were just practicing. Russia ordered all residents to leave Chechnya and warned the U.S. of its nuclear capability. Who would intervene?

The United States: planetary policeman

Although we would like to believe we can sit down at the table, man to man, woman to woman, and hammer out an agreement that works, one acceptable to both sides, alas, there are many sides; and human beings generally fail to come to agreement, even for their own families, let alone for the planet. We presently have enough nuclear weapons in existence on the planet to blow it up seventeen times. So if the planet still needs to be policed, a prevailing "piano top," I, for one, prefer the police action of the United States over any other. I say this with deep regret, having been one of those, from the belly, blaring out "We Are the World, We Are the Children." We still are.

Education deteriorated - grow worse

The state of our education is equally discouraging. Great deterioration occurred when school systems started grabbing on to piano tops to improve the pedagogical methods of teachers: Whole word reading system, new math, bilingual education. Schools in the United States are producing graduates who are illiterate, the "dumbing of America." How did it come to be? For one thing, we have ignored the basics. My grandmother, with an eighth grade education in a one-room school house, was better educated than most high school graduates and even many college graduates.

Reading

Our children cannot read. Schools in California are just now returning to phonics after losing a decade of students with the whole word reading system. This return to phonics presents us with another unanticipated problem, a generation of teachers who themselves never learned phonics, who have to be re-educated in order to teach the basics. This is not an issue of money. The city of Inglewood, at the bottom of the economic hierarchy, has managed to achieve higher scores on standardized tests than Beverly Hills, just by returning to basic phonics.

Math

Our students cannot do basic math. Elementary school teachers in California are currently meeting a requirement to study beginning algebra after school or during vacations. Why? They weren't required to take math as part of their preparation to be teachers, and now they find themselves incompetent to meet basic standards of instruction.

Bilingual education

Our immigrant students are confused. The immigrants who came to the United States in the eighteenth and nineteenth century abandoned their old language and learned English. It was their ticket to success in their adopted land. We thought in the last half of the twentieth century that we could improve the performance of immigrants by teaching them first in their native tongue. It didn't work. We've returned to immersion.

Quick fixes

Nothing improved by grabbing on to these piano tops. Students graduate from our high schools without an understanding of the language they are expected to speak and to write, without a basic knowledge of adding, subtracting, and the multiplication tables.

The California State University at Long Beach reported in the fall of 1999 that remedial work would be required in both English and Math for at least half of the entering students. My students who learn English as a second language have a better grounding in English grammar than the native-born speakers of English who graduated from our schools. My native speakers didn't have the benefit of Miss Ruth Sherman who drilled the rules so thoroughly into my memory that I still can recite them by rote.

Teachers untaught

Most teachers teaching today never learned the rules. My Asian immigrant students find college-level math classes easy. Why? They mastered the rudiments in elementary school and high school. Here memorizing the multiplication tables was abandoned for calculators. The graduates of high school are so dependent upon calculators that they can't perform simple problems in their heads, can't even make change when the cash register computer is down. When we grabbed on to calculators as lifesavers, we forgot that they were originally programmed by human beings who told them what to do. We need to put more emphasis on memorization, on honing and perfecting the capacity of the original computer, our human brain.

Language an industrial tool.

Fuller distinguishes between the original tool and the industrial tool. If a man uses a gourd to carry water, he has created a tool. If two men together use a tool, it becomes an industrial tool. Thus, our language is an industrial tool, beginning with our first grunt, our first symbolic cave figure. Basic knowledge of how these industrial tools work should be the core of our education system. When we grab on to alternatives, we produce outcomes that rob people of their right to maximize the experience of the early years devoted exclusively to school. When you see the frantic clerk, lost without a calculator, counting on his fingers, you recognize a return to the basics, to one of man's earliest tools.

Skewed values

We have a nation with completely skewed values. Young people preparing for a teaching career are discouraged because "there's no money in that," yet athletes are paid millions of dollars for chasing after a ball. My son-in-law is committed to teaching adolescents in underprivileged areas. He is a self-made man who left a troublesome home to join the Marines, was promoted to sergeant in the Marine Corp, trained as a cryptologist, served in Desert Storm, and earned both a B.A. and a M.A. His starting salary as a biology teacher was $31,000. His career is a monetary family sacrifice. Isn't this deplorable? We need the brightest and best teaching our students, serving as role models. When we put the money into our schools, often the administration takes care of itself, and the funds never make their way into classroom instruction and teacher support. There is an enormous gap between the intent of the people and the implementation of the bureaucracy.

Governmental dysfunction

The gap between the intent of the people and the actual implementation in government demonstrates that it shares equal time with education as an institutionalized piano top. Since attorneys have the greatest facility with the language, spend years learning to manipulate the truth, and practice delivery of deception with sincerity, it evolved that they began to "run" for public office and then made an institution of it. We long ago left behind the farmers, the merchants, and the makers who came together to frame the Constitution of the United States. For them public service was a duty that they would accept for a short term to serve their nation, an inconvenience they would tolerate in exchange for the exercise of the right of freedom.

Masters of manipulation indebted to special interests

We return to the polls, that is, usually less than half of the registered voters, to elect and re-elect to public office self-made masters of verbal manipulation. Then we complain that our problems are not being solved. We put people in a position to make decisions about finance, agriculture, building projects, health care, and industry who have never met a payroll, never constructed a building, never built a road, never treated a patient, never invented nor manufactured anything. I know of only one medical doctor in all of Congress.

Our public officials are influenced in their decisions by the lobbyists who mold them and make them, and by big-money corporate backers who fund their campaigns, great pirates. The national conventions of both parties in the year 2000 were hosted to extravagant gala events by the lobbyists. Certainly, they must expect a return on the investment. Even when the heads of the parties articulate a plan for America worth fighting for, we all know that the gap between intent and execution is wide and long. Special interests too frequently prevail. Bill Gates defied the system when he ignored the lobby procedure and went to Washington, D.C. to defend himself in his anti-trust case. The judge paid him back. In Washington it is either "their way" or the highway.

Institutional practices replicated in personal choices

When we examine the institutionalized piano tops that we accept as normal and seldom question, it's little wonder that we each do the same thing in our personal lives. We cling to jobs, to relationships, to organizations, to systems of belief, long after they have ceased to serve us. Why do we do this? Often it is inertia. Change requires too much energy. Often it is fear, fear that if we let go of the piano top, the better lifesaver or the real lifesaver may not show up. So long as we cling to the old piano top, there's no space for the real thing. Thus, the trap is set.

Trap distinguished from solution

How can we distinguish a trap from a solution or an opportunity? A trap creates the same results over and over without ever solving the problem and without space for growth and change. How do we get out of the trap? Open the trap door. Where is this trap door? It's in our minds, in our thoughts. We may think it's in our wallets and purses, in our beds or on our kitchen tables, or in the restaurant where we eat breakfast every morning; but it's in our thinking. Emerson claims, "There is a crack in everything God has made." That means we still have a chance.

Reality determined by thought

Here is an example of how our thoughts determine our reality. I recall showing a home to a gentleman with knee problems who wanted to sell his tri-level home and move to a single story home. For several years he had been confined to a few rooms in his house because he couldn't go up and down the stairs. The home we visited was in a quiet, well-kept neighborhood behind a code-operated gate. The owner was a fastidious housekeeper and creative decorator, so it was attractive and inviting. The gentleman liked the home, in fact, wanted to know if the owner would sell the furniture because he acknowledged he could never decorate so effectively on his own.

Then began his doubts and fears. Q=question; A=answer; O=observation:

Buyer:

Q: How can my friends drop in to visit me?

Realtor:

A: Oh, just give them the code to the gate.

Realtor:

Q: Do your friends usually drop over without calling first?

Buyer:

A: Well, actually hardly anyone just drops by. But my gardener has to get in once a week.

Buyer:

O: Besides, my friends won't feel comfortable in such a nice house.

Realtor:

Q: Will you feel at home in this house?

Buyer:

A: I've never lived in such a nice house.

Realtor:

Q: This is a small neighborhood, and the people get along well. You probably would make some new friends.

A: Actually, I've been alone for a long time. I don't really have many friends.

Vulnerability of the unknown
House a shell

My job as a realtor is to listen so that I can help people find the home where they will be comfortable and happy. The cost of this home was not an issue, because this gentleman's present home, which he inhabited only partially, finally sold for more than this one. He liked this house, yet articulated a fear that if he let go of his current way of living, he would lose his friendships.

No decision a decision

But in the end, the friendships weren't the issue. The house represented to him a new way of life, a new kind of being, a new self-image; and if he let go of what he had, he would leave himself open to the unknown, and he would move out of his comfort zone. This is vulnerability. The choice of a home is emotional, and making that choice is a kind of exposure. He resolved the problem that day with inertia; he didn't make a decision. Someone else put in an offer the same day and got the house. No decision is a decision. Incidentally, we did find him the right home eventually, and he made his move. It was, however, an emotional roller coaster.

Walls man-created

We hang on to piano tops because we fear vulnerability, we fear any change in the *status quo*; and we prefer inertia to decisiveness. Events may force change. During the first half of the 1990's, after Gorbachev took down a symbolic piano top, the Berlin Wall, the State of California was in disarray. For almost half a century we had created a defense mythos based on what the Berlin Wall was walling in: The Soviet Union, the giant monster with its missiles aimed at the U.S. A major portion of the U.S. defense industry operation was located in California. When the wall came down, it was apparent to the general public that the Soviet Union was weaker than we had believed, that Communism had failed, that an idea more than a reality had dominated our U.S. budget and defense spending. A cartoon read, "Will the last Communist please turn out the lights." We might even have reason to suspect that our lawyer-run government took advantage of the wall to mobilize our defense spending and to keep the economy rolling.

Sudden loss

When that same government acted in sudden haste to cut defense spending, without the foresight to re-direct that spending to the multitude of domestic problems needing solutions, many of the best-trained aerospace engineers in the world were put out of work. Along with them went their support personnel. This decision affected everyone in California: builders, bankers, grocers, dry cleaners, car salesmen, mechanics, retailers, realtors, clergymen, psychologists, educators. Those who provided homes, things, food, and toys lost or went out of business. Those who provided helping services picked up. This was true especially for education.

Education in bad economy

When the economy is bad, people go back to school. As an educator I found my classes filled with deposed aerospace engineers and other employees affected by the downsizing who were coming back to school to train for different professions. I cannot recall a single instance when the individual, the displaced worker, wasn't actually relieved. Usually he had been dissatisfied with his job for years, but he couldn't give it up because he had been living on the edge: his kids were in school, his house payments were high, his car payments covered several vehicles, his retirement was just a few years away. He was trapped by responsibilities.

Letting go, letting in.

The loss of jobs freed displaced and downsized workers to explore aspects of themselves that they had stifled in their previous work. These people became teachers, counselors, entrepreneurs; and they are much happier today. In almost every instance, even though they saw the purge coming, they couldn't let go, not until their frozen fingers were dislodged from the piano top. I particularly recall one gentleman who had built missiles for Rockwell, earning a salary of $65,000 a year. He had disliked his work for ten years, but he was trapped by his income. His true love was coaching, which he had done on the side. He used this opportunity to get a teaching credential, to follow his heart. His greatest worry, whether his daughter would be able to go to college, was eliminated by his loss of income. She now qualified for a scholarship.

Forced renewal

Let me not paint too rosy a picture of this process. This forced vulnerability from the downsizing, the social euphemism for getting fired, was cataclysmic. Most spent the first six months to a year in depression, guilt, and fear, paralyzed by the shock of the event. Homes were lost, cars were lost, children were forced to drop out of college. Everyone in the family took a hit. Family members started to lay blame, to get angry and hostile. Divorces occurred. The forced renewal, reconstruction, rediscovery was at great price. Emerson sums it up with this observation:

> Our strength grows out of our weakness. The indignation which arms itself with secret forces does not awaken until we

are pricked and stung and sorely assailed. A great man is always willing to be little. Whilst he sits on the cushion of advantages, he goes to sleep. When he is pushed, tormented, defeated, he has a chance to learn something; he has been put on his wits, on his manhood; he has gained facts; learns his ignorance; is cured of the insanity of conceit; has got moderation and real skill. [3]

It takes courage to let go of comfort and security, even if what you are doing isn't using your talents and abilities. We stay attached to a piano top long after it ceases to be challenging or even financially rewarding out of fear of the unknown. The people whom I described above had all redefined their purpose and had begun to work within a year after they lost their jobs. If they had been able to see into the future, they could have taken a vacation.

Gone fishing!

Fuller, in fact, advocates replacing unemployment with fishing fellowships. He would "give each human who is or becomes unemployed a life fellowship in research development or in just simple thinking. Man must be able to dare to think truthfully and to act accordingly without fear of losing his franchise to live."[4] By his calculation, if we had 100,000 people on fishing fellowships, that is just fishing and thinking, one brilliant idea would generate enough income to pay for the 99,999 other fellowships.

Indecision: seedling of fear

Fear holds us back from truly knowing who we are or what we can do. When we are afraid, our intuition gets blocked and can't get through to us. Napoleon Hill regards indecision, doubt, and fear as a package: "Indecision is the seedling of fear!...Indecision crystallizes into doubt, the two blend and become fear! The blending process often is slow. This is one reason why these three enemies are so dangerous. They germinate and grow *without their presence being observed*."[5] The concept of a piano top is a vehicle for moving beyond that fear to take action.

CL's Story

One of my students, I will call him CL, provides an example. He came to the United States from Hong Kong where he ran his own advertising business. He wanted to leave Hong Kong before China took it over. When he first arrived in the United States, he took a job as a messenger for minimum wage. As his language skills improved and he gained more confidence, CL worked his way into a comfortable quality control position in a stable computer firm. His son is now a teenager, bright and college-bound. When it became apparent that CL, as head of the family, would need a degree to move on to a better job to support the family endeavors, he began taking classes at our local community colleges. He took my class at the recommendation of his speech teacher who told him he might benefit from my instruction in ways that would go well beyond the improvement of his writing skills.

The job offer

Almost simultaneously with his enrollment in my class, CL had a job offer from another local firm. It offered higher pay but more responsibility and more leadership expectations. He first told me that he had decided not to take the job offer because he had seniority in his present company, knew the job well, and needed security for his family. After we spent a class session on "piano tops," he said he was going to spend the next week thinking about the new opportunity. Finally, he decided to take the risk and make the change, to let go of his piano top. Although he was competent in his work in quality control, he knew it used only a small part of his ability.

The right choice

CL came back after his first week on the new job absolutely ecstatic. Not only did it offer opportunities for his personal growth and professional advancement beyond his expectations; but also, during his training, he discovered that his new company, Kingston Technology, was started by John Tu and David Sun who had divided a $100,000,000 bonus among their employees in 1996 when they sold eighty percent of their company to Softbank Corp. Although CL arrived too late to be a recipient of that bonus, he felt privileged to work for such a company. Soon after he made his change, Kingston announced a $20,000,000 bonus to be distributed over the next ten years following a buyback. That same company has initiated a program to encourage entrepreneurs within the corporation to start up new companies, offering legal aid, seed money, and office space to approved projects. CL is absolutely jubilant that he had the courage to let go of the piano top and to trust his ability.

Relationships: emotionally charged vulnerability

When we come to the primary relationships in our lives, we are dealing with issues that may seem over-simplified by a symbolic "piano top." That is, however, precisely why the concept works so effectively. It isn't emotionally charged; it is neutral. When we examine a relationship, directly, head-on, we get sidetracked by our feelings or by a sense of obligation. Always with a piano top we are asking, "Is this a permanent solution or is it a temporary life-saver?"

Star equilibrium

D. H. Lawrence described the ideally balanced permanent solution as "star equilibrium." In a relationship between two lovers, when "star equilibrium" is achieved, each individual is as a star, occupies its own orbit, has its own light, and has its own energy. When the two stars come together, the light is exchanged, a brighter light shines forth, and a greater energy is created. Each star then is empowered to shine brighter within its own orbit. Do not feel bad if your star lacks a little luster. This ideal is seldom achieved by Lawrence's characters in his novels, yet the very idea of "star equilibrium," once articulated, becomes a possibility. Anything less is a piano top.

Stuck in the condition

Once a piano top is defined, it has a reality of its own. It can facilitate the process of "letting go" or "getting out of" a relationship that has become a trap. The trap is particularly powerful when the relationship fits definitions that might be addressed in support groups and by 12-step programs, for instance co-dependence or victimization. I am not denigrating the work of such programs. These programs and groups do, however, focus on the condition; and when all we can think about is the condition and how it affects our life, it is very difficult to free our thought to find a solution, or to find a better way to live and love. When we look at our life from inside the problem we've labeled, we get stuck in the condition and can't get far enough away to ask the important question, "Is this working for my greatest good?"

Love ignition — to set a fire

The bottom line in a relationship between two people is loving and being loved. The exchange of love ignites our star. When that isn't happening, then it isn't working for our greatest good. One of my students, for instance, was in a relationship with a woman who borrowed money from him, always with excuses of losing her job or getting sick or helping her family. He finally discovered she had a drug addiction problem, and she was using the money for cocaine. Another student discovered that her boyfriend of seven years, to whom she considered herself "engaged," had been cheating on her with another woman for the past three years.

Separate and neutral

The "piano top" concept worked for them precisely because of its separation and neutrality. A piano top is not involved in outcomes. A piano top, used appropriately in a relationship, merely serves as a temporary vehicle to bring two people together for companionship, perhaps intimacy. A mature, lasting, loving relationship must have an inner integrity to support and sustain it. Each of these people, by asking the hard question, was able to see that the callous deception, use, and abuse practiced by the partner totally obliterated any possibility for such integrity. It was obvious that to continue to cling to the relationship for any reason was wasting time and resources.

The hard questions

We get clear, unmuddled answers when we ask the hard questions. Is this a rewarding situation? Or has a temporary lifesaver been adopted permanently through habit, or neglect, or fear that I'm just not good enough for something better? The definition of insanity is doing the things we've always done expecting different results. Knowledge is power. When we ask ourselves these basic questions about our work, about our friends, about our affiliations, about our primary relationships, we can get clear. These questions should have positive affirmation.

The right orbit

Suppose you ask, "Does this relationship/job/organization energize me, inspire me, ignite me, invigorate me, empower me?" It is not working if the response is this: "It boxes me in, subdues me, stifles me, suppresses me." It's a piano top. There should be no discrepancy between the "who I am" within it and the "who I am" apart from it. The same star occupies the orbit, joins with another star outside its orbit, and then moves back into its own.

Dependence and symbiosis

The following exercises are for self-examination to help you determine where you stand tall and where you stoop, where you are self-sufficient, and where you are attached, where you are free and where you are trapped. Remember, there is a difference between dependence and symbiosis. In dependency one side is clinging to the other and cannot sustain itself alone. In symbiosis, both sides can function independently, but they come together because it is to their advantage. They function more successfully together than apart. This term has biological roots referring to two species of organisms, such as a fungus and alga, which together make a lichen.

Piano top conversion

Don't expect perfect clarity, black and white. The subtle ambiguity of life makes it interesting. You will probably discover there are elements of empowerment and elements of suppression in your relationships. This does not mean that you need to throw out the baby with the bath. It may mean that you need to examine what serves you and what doesn't, and then to ask how it could change. In other words, you may be able to convert a piano top to a workable model of a life-saver with just a few modifications, perhaps with something so simple as an earnest and sincere conversation with your significant other or your boss.

On the following pages, you will find the main categories of your life with places for you to fill in people, institutions and things. *People* may include your primary relationship, your parents or siblings, your children, your friends, your colleagues or associates, your employer. *Institutions* may be the company you work for, your church, your school, your service clubs or affiliate organizations. *Things* may be food or drink, toys, or activities. Include sources of recreation and revitalization under *things*.

Choice verbs and adjectives

In each instance, ask yourself, how does this serve me? What are the ways it could improve? Here are some adjectives you may find useful to add to your own list: empowered, supported, reinforced, energized, encouraged, inhibited, reserved, stymied, confined, trapped. Notice that each of these adjectives is derived from a verb. The more we verb our life, the more vital it becomes. The only words in our language of real importance are verbs, for in them resides the action or way of being that defines our life: to be, to know, to feel, to give, to take, to accept, to love, to engender, to create, to investigate, to determine, to go, to come, to consider, to fear, to believe.

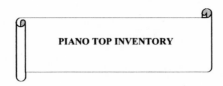

PIANO TOP INVENTORY

List below the "piano tops" you have clung to in your lifetime, temporary lifesavers that you may have made permanent. Next to the piano top, write down the reason you made that choice.

PIANO TOP	REASON FOR CHOICE
RELATIONSHIPS:	
JOBS:	

PIANO TOP	REASON FOR CHOICE
THINGS: Lifestyle Choices—Spiritual and Physical	

Are there patterns that you observe: similar attractions, similar anxieties, similar avoidance?

_____

_____

_____

_____

_____

_____

_____

Midway along the journey of our life
I woke to find myself in some dark woods,
For I had wandered off from the straight path.

How hard it is to tell what it was like,
This wood of wilderness, savage and stubborn
(the thought of it brings back all my old fear),

A bitter place! Death could scarce be bitterer.
But if I would show the good that came of it
I must talk about things other than the good.
Dante, *Inferno*[1]

These roses under my window make no reference to former roses or to
better ones; they are for what they are; they exist with God to-day.
There is no time to them. There is simply the rose; it is perfect in every
moment of its existence. Before a leaf-bud has burst, its whole life acts;
in the full-blown flower there is no more; in the leafless root there is no
less. Its nature is satisfied and it satisfies nature all in moments alike.
But man postpones or remembers; he does not live in the present, but
with reverted eye laments the past, or, heedless of the riches that sur-
round him, stands on tiptoe to foresee the future.

Emerson, Self Reliance [2]

No Mistakes

Only Opportunities to Discover the Truth

The Tiger and the Goats
Giving birth

An ancient animal fable, one the late mythologist, Joseph Campbell, tells again and again, is the story about a female tiger and her unborn son. The mother is pregnant, just about to deliver, and for various reasons has been without food for several days. She is absolutely starving. She comes out of the jungle onto a grassy meadow, and there right in front of her, she sees a herd of goats eating grass. She thinks to her self, "Ah ha! Here is what I need." Her heart starts to beat, the adrenalin courses through her burdensome body, and with great fervor, she pounces upon the goat closest to her. She gives it all of the force she has left, and in the strenuous act gives birth to a baby tiger and dies.

Adopted baby

The frightened goats all scatter, but when they realize that the imminent danger has passed, that the drama has ceased, they come back to the scene of attack. There they find there the dead mother tiger and the baby tiger. Now goats are givers of milk, they are great nurturers, and they have great parental instincts. It goes against their nature to abandon the little baby tiger to predators like his mother, so they adopt him. One of the mother goats nurses the little tiger until he is strong and mature enough to have real food. They raise him as one of

164

themselves, as a goat. He learns to eat grass and to bleat. As he approaches adolescence, he has a slightly confused demeanor, but most adolescents do, and no one in the herd thinks much about it.

The big male tiger and the baby

One day an enormous male tiger, very hungry, comes upon the herd of goats, and all of the goats scatter. But the little tiger, because he is a tiger and not a goat, stays.

The big fellow looks at the little fellow, and he says, "What are you doing here with these goats? You're a tiger."

And the little fellow looks at him, says, "Baaah," and takes a little nibble of grass.

The big fellow thinks what to do next, so he decides to give the little tiger a visual lesson. He takes the neck of the little tiger in his mouth and carries him to a pond, totally still, and sets the little fellow down where he can see himself.

"Now," he says, "Just look at you. You aren't a goat. You're a tiger."

The little fellow looks, says, "Baaah," and takes another nibble of grass.

The big fellow can't stand this grazing and Baahing," so he says to himself, "What I need to do is to get this little tiger out of this meadow.

The little tiger's tigerness

He picks the little one up by the neck again and carries him off to his den. Strewn all over his den are the remains of the gazelle he had just killed and eaten. They are lying all around, and the smell of the fresh blood from the kill nauseates the little fellow.

"Here," the big male tiger says to the little fellow, offering him a big, bloody chunk, "Have some."

The little fellow says, "Baah, I'm a vegetarian."

Now this big male tiger is getting more than a bit impatient with this sassy little sissy. So he says, "You are a tiger, and tigers eat gazelles. And he grabs a hunk of gazelle meal and forces the chunk down the little fellow's throat.

The digestion of the gazelle meat warms the innards of the little fellow. He feels a power and vitality moving though his body as he awakens to instincts within himself, long dormant. His blood begins to flow, and he feels fire and passion, feelings he never had before. He lets out his first, little tiger roar. It feels so good, he does it again, only louder and more powerful.

" Now," says the big fellow, "You are a tiger. Go into the forest and be who you are."

Mistaken identity

It is obvious from this story that all along this little fellow was a tiger among goats. He just didn't know it. His hanging out with goats had nothing to do with his actual tigerness. At the appropriate opportunity, with the right leadership, he saw who he really was. The tiger had been there all the time and was ready to express itself.

Doing, Discovering, and Discarding

When I was in kindergarten, someone told me, probably the boy next door, that I could make paste with flowers and water. So, I went out into the back yard, and I plucked the blossoms off from my mother's petunias. I chopped up the blossoms, added water, and then applied this fragrant paste to two pieces of paper. It didn't work. The papers came right apart. When mother came home and found her garden stripped of its flowers, she was not happy. I was equally distressed because my paste was not sticking. I explained to her that I was just trying to make paste. She informed me I had the wrong kind of *flower*; I needed to mix *flour* with water. What a blunder! So I quickly got some flour out of the cupboard, mixed it with water, and lo and behold, I made paste. It stuck.

Misdirection to mastery

As I look back on this experiment, I see that I learned not only a scientific lesson about adhesion, what makes things stick; but also I learned about the language, about words that sound alike but have different meanings, homonyms. It also is a lesson about how our actions are guided by words. Two infinitive phrases in the English language misdirect our thinking: "to try" and "to make mistakes." Nothing was ever accomplished by trying. We accomplish by doing. A mistake, by this way of thinking, is merely what we *mis* took as a truth. We cannot actually make mistakes; we can only temporarily misapprehend a truth, take something as a truth until we discover that it isn't and something else is. I think of it as three Ds: **Doing, Discovering**, and **Discarding**.

This is how we learn to cope and to master all aspects of living: to approach someone, to accomplish a task, to prepare a meal, to manufacture a product, to design a home, to drive a car, to ride a bicycle, to behave in a relationship, to overcome fear or anxiety, to express love, to deliver a lecture, to teach a class, to read a poem, to write a novel or screenplay, to wash a dog, to care for a baby. Our life is a continual process of practicing the three D's: **Doing, Discovering,** and **Discarding.**

Man's two tools

R. Buckminster Fuller observes two kinds of tools developed by man: 1) The craft tool which could be invented by one man all alone in the wilderness; 2) The industrial tool which requires more than one man. By this definition, the spoken word, which requires the presence and communication of two men, was the first industrial tool. From Fuller's perspective: "The Bible says, 'In the beginning was the word'; I say to you, 'In the beginning of industrialization was the spoken word.' With the graphic writing of the words and ideas we have the beginning of the computer for the computer stores and retrieves information. The written word, dictionary and the book were the first information storing and retrieving system." [3]

The written word: the first computer

By this definition man has been designing the computer since the first symbolic representation made on the wall of a cave. Man alone expresses himself in symbols. This is the divine synergy of the human race: When two or more are gathered together the outcome is greater than the potential production of one man alone. In January of 1999, a team of German archeologists discovered a clay tablet in Egypt in the tomb of King Scorpion the First which they believe, by present knowledge, to be the first written word. It is called the "Mountain of Light," and the message conveyed involves taxes, linen and oil. They date this *circa* 3300 B.C. If this is true, it has been just a mere 5300 years from the first computer scratched on a clay tablet to our present technological capability. That is just a mere speck of time in the history of our universe and our planet. The "Mountain of Light" is integrated into the graphic design reflected on the cover of this book. We note well our human concerns have altered little in over 5000 years. We are still talking about oil, taxes, and linen, ie. mummies-death.

Revising truth

We have come a long way in our acceptance of the process of discovery, i.e. uncovering error, and revision, i.e., revising what we see as true. We anticipate that each day our research will bring us closer to understanding the way things work, but we know that what is true today will inevitably be revised tomorrow. For instance, Celera Corporation and the National Institute of Health separately and then cooperatively worked on decoding the human genome. This genome has inscribed upon it all of the human genes, each gene causing one or more instruction. The genome is thus the full DNA tape, the operating manual for the cell, with 60,000-100,000 genes. As research unfolds, each new discovery will revise our thinking, revise our theories, and revise our practices in treating illness and disease.

The climate of opinion today accepts the idea that today's "truth" will be tomorrow's "mistake," something we *mis*-took as the truth. On a recent Friday, three announcements of discoveries were made by totally separate scientific investigation teams: the enzyme in the protein that causes Alzheimer's Disease; a possible vaccine against prostate cancer; a possible vaccine against colon cancer. The more we know about the genetic basis for conditions and how the genes work, the better we will be able to eradicate disease, deformity, dysfunction. We are in a whirlwind of discarding old ideas, former conclusions, and previous ways of solving problems. We anticipate that each discovery will lead to future ones. We hold in esteem those uniquely endowed people who are at the forefront of scientific investigation, and we acknowledge the role of the computer in accelerating this process.

The new Rose Center for Earth and Space of the American Museum of Natural History in New York City walks us through 13 billion years as we enter. We are struck with how briefly human life has been here, that just 240,000 years ago dinosaurs roamed, and that half of the knowledge of the universe has been compiled since 1985. Anticipating present beliefs will be discarded for new discoveries, the walk can be changed and updated. How differently we think from the time of Copernicus and Galileo!

Social lag-time: ethical dilemmas

The progressive discovery, re-evaluation, rejection, and re-discovery of pure scientific truth is easier for us to deal with than the social, cultural, philosophical, and spiritual ramifications of our growing knowledge; for ethical decisions will need to be made. Today we anticipate the defining of the humane genome, bringing increased understanding of the genes and the orders that those genes deliver to the human system. Next comes the application of that knowledge. How do we use it?

Do we create perfect human beings? Do we decide what model of perfection we prefer and get rid of the rest of us? Who, then, is ok, and who isn't? Who decides? If we can eliminate violent personalities right out of existence, shouldn't we do it? Is that what God means for us to do? Do we turn it over to the lawyers we elect to public office? They are trained to manipulate words and distort truth, to make the means serve their own ends. Whom do we trust? Should we let the Pope decide? Since born-again Christians do not consider Catholics to be Christians, what right does that give the Pope? Maybe the Muslims should decide. They are the fastest growing religion. Should we just leave it to Beaver?

Bumps in the road

We are at the threshold; and our road of life, while spectacular in its potential, is nevertheless perilous. Our common vernacular has phrases for this: bumps in the road, dead ends, wrong turns, curves, off the beaten path, pitfalls along the way, off the map, off the chart, derailed. They all assume the right direction is going from point A to point B; and they all assume that, although there is a road to discovery, it is marked with error. Many of our most compelling human spiritual stories, stories we tell again and again for inspiration, have to do with a lost man who sees the light. As Joseph Campbell has observed, human beings have a hard time communing with perfection. We can come directly to the broken and wounded Christ.

Down in the depths before the light

We must know the worst about ourselves before we are allowed to acknowledge the best about ourselves. This so often occurs allegorically along the road of life. The apostle, Paul, sees the light on the road from Tarsus. The poet, Dante, loses his way and ends up in the Dark Wood, the dark night of the soul. His vision of the *Divine Comedy*, the progress of man's soul, proceeds from eternal darkness in the inferno, through purgatory and into paradise. In the medieval *Piers the Plowman*, the dreamer sees a vision of a high tower, Truth, and a deep dungeon, Wrong. The Seven Deadly Sins, the carnal curse, must be purged before the pilgrim can seek St. Truth.

In John Bunyan's *Pilgrim's Progress,* Christian flees the City of Destruction and begins his pilgrimage to the Celestial city. Among his many stops and encounters along the way, he passes through the Slough of Despond, the Valley of Humiliation, and the Valley of the Shadow of Death. Finally, the Giant Despair must be overcome before he may have his beatific vision. Gerard Manley Hopkins, the converted Catholic priest who found his parish assignment in Ireland such a trial, proclaims in one of his sonnets written during a period of despair, "Oh the mind, mind has mountains,/Cliffs of Fall. / Hold them lightly he who has never been there."

Oedipus: *The unconscious mistake*

The tragic character

Aristotle defines the tragic character as one who is basically good, but who, through excess, too much of a good thing, falls into error. Aristotle based his analysis of the perfect drama in his *Poetics* on the play, *Oedipus Rex,* by Sophocles. This play demonstrates the three unities: time, place, and action. The time is one twenty-four hour period; the place is outside the king's palace in Thebes; the action is Oedipus' discovery of his real identity, the truth about himself.

The city in plague

Oedipus is the most conscientious of kings. His city and his people are suffering from the siege of a plague. People are dying, sick, unable to work. No children are being born. He has come to speak directly to his people, not through emissaries: "I

Oedipus whom all men call the Great."[4] He tells his people that he will get to the bottom of the cause of the plague; he will leave no stone unturned. He is the man you would want to lead your corporation, your organization, not isolated in his office surrounded by upper management, but out on the floor, zealous, curious and persistent.

The zealous search for truth

Oedipus has sent his brother-in-law, Creon, to consult with the oracle, Phoebus Apollo. Creon reports that Phoebus says he must find the murderer of the former king, Laius, whose wife, Jocasta, in now Oedipus' wife. Oedipus announces that he will drive this person from the land. He calls Tiresias, the prophet. Tiresias does not want to speak, for he knows the truth Oedipus seeks. Oedipus gets angry, their tempers flare, and Tiresias, pushed to the wall tells him "You are the land's pollution!"[5] Oedipus, whose tragic flaw is often called *hubris*, self-pride, begins to call people in, each messenger bringing a fresh clue, each one uncovering the need for more information.

With dreadful irony, Sophocles contrasts the darkness and the light. Each discovery Oedipus makes, each fact he uncovers about apparent circumstances, each new bit of evidence that illuminates and brings the truth closer to the light, leads Oedipus more deeply into the darkness of his own character. The awful truth is that Oedipus, on his way to Thebes, killed an old man at a crossroad where three roads meet. This was Laius. Oedipus did not know it was his father, for he believed himself to be the son of the King of Corinth. He is married to his mother, Jocasta. He has fathered three incestuous children. Jocasta hangs herself. Oedipus is the victim of the curse of the Gods on the House of Laius. Yet he fulfills the decree of exile he declared against the polluter of the land as the responsible and heroic man he is. Oedipus takes the brooch from Jocasta's dress and blinds himself, puts out his eyes. He leaves his city in self-exile.

The oracle is fulfilled.

This had all been foretold, that the son of Laius would murder his father and sleep with his mother. When Jocasta gave birth to a son, she was ordered by Laius, her husband and king, to abandon the child, the baby Oedipus, in the wilderness to die. Jocasta, instead, gave the child to a shepherd, who in turn gave the child to the king and queen of Corinth who raised him. When Oedipus, in adolescence, overheard that he had a curse upon him, that he was to murder his father and marry his mother, he ran away to avoid it, believing that the king and queen of Corinth were his real parents. He met Laius at a crossroad where three roads meet. Both had tempers, they got in a fight, and Oedipus killed Laius. Oedipus then went on to Thebes where the sphinx held the city under siege. He solved the riddle of the sphinx: What walks on four legs in the morning, two at noon, and three at sundown? The answer is "Man," who crawls as a child, stands upright at his prime, and walks with a cane in old age. Oedipus' reward was to marry the queen, Jocasta.

The Oedipus complex

Freud made this Oedipal situation the basis for the Oedipus complex. When Oedipus, in Sophocles' play, tells Jocasta about the curse he heard in Corinth, that he would kill his father and marry his mother, Jocasta soothes him by saying this is something men do in their dreams. Freud took Jocasta's words to define the Oedipus complex. Freud's psychoanalysis, rooted in the interpretation of dreams, as in the play, brings the buried darkness to light. The "collective unconscious" defined by Karl Jung is also in darkness. We bring it to light in order to understand ourselves. That which we shroud in darkness is error. We fear it.

Fear of error: race consciousness.

The myth underlying the Oedipus story, the action of Sophocles' play, the basic tenet of Freud's psychoanalysis and Jung's collective unconscious, all have one thing in common, the human fear of being or acting in error. I consider it part of our race consciousness. In our western world, it is associated with the idea of sin. The word sinister has its roots in the Latin *sinstra*, meaning left. "Left" is the opposite of "right." It is good to be right handed; it is good to be right.

Error punished

It is wrong to be in error. We impart it to our children by demanding perfection. We punish them if they bring home papers from school marked up with red ink. We take away privileges. Mother put my bicycle in the garage. We may not even know that we are sending the message so powerfully, that we may be delivering a sentence. My daughter, for instance, used to hide her report cards, wouldn't bring them home. If I asked, she would say she didn't get one. In retrospect, I realize that her older brother's obsession for perfection, his pride in his report cards, and my praise of him for it, made her feel that if she had anything less than perfection, it wasn't good enough. I didn't mean to send that message, to sentence her in that way, not consciously. *But* I did.

All powerful But

But is the most powerful word in the English language. It eradicates all that went before it. Nothing eludes its power. The roses Emerson describes beneath his windows know no *but*. They are satisfied, perfect at every stage, at each unfoldment of their natural growth. There is nothing in the consciousness of a rose of right or wrong, good or evil. The rose just is. It knows no shame or guilt. It makes no apologies. People, on the other hand, beat themselves up because of error. They regret the past, mock the present, and fear the future. They hold up for themselves an image of perfection that is contrary to the natural principle of growth.

No truth without error

So here we are again with the paradox. Everything that we know about how our planet works was discovered by making mistakes. In the scientific method, a name applied to a process we developed pragmatically to test our hunches, the mistakes, the errors, the erroneously formulated conclusions, are absolutely essential to discovery of truth. It's like a swimmer doing the breast stroke, with each movement of the arms pushing away the dead weight of wrong answers in order to move forward to the right answer.

No winner without a loser

The intellectual process demands the mistakes. The psychological, social, emotional judgment that we apply to ourselves when we make mistakes, comes from a race consciousness demanding error-proof performance. It reminds me of the ambiguity of my own self-absorbed sentence. We want our children to compete, yet in every competition it is inevitable there will be a winner and a loser. We tell them to be "good losers," but we also let them know by the other 93% of our communication that "nobody loves a loser."

Mistakes: a psychological impulse

The cover story in *Money* magazine, September 1999, was entitled "Investors Biggest Mistakes." The author, Rob Turner, is perplexed by this: "Particularly vexing is that investors should, in theory, be making fewer mistakes these days. There are more ways than ever to research, monitor and manage your finances, whether through discount brokers, a flood of financial publications, constant television coverage or the Internet. But though the investing world may have changed, people haven't; our errors remain remarkably similar. That's because the psychological impulses behind many of our mistakes remain the same."[6]

Throwing good money after bad

We may treat a windfall frivolously, or we may "throw good money after bad," just because we hate losing money more than we like getting it. And, like Oedipus, we may suffer from *hubris*, self-pride. One woman "skipped the research" and took a tip from a friend who claimed to have insider information about a take-over; another woman "skipped the research" and took her boyfriend's advice. One gentleman was so afraid of risk that he put his entire retirement fund in fixed income and ended up with far less than his colleagues; one couple took a flier on a stock listed on the Yahoo message board; and one woman invested her money in a high-yield limited partnership and then discovered she couldn't liquidate it to make the down payment on a house. Motley fool, we need you!

Distinguish blunders from mistakes

A scandal erupted early in the year 2000 when two investors who had invested with a firm located in Orange County in California filed to force an investment firm, DFJ Italia, Ltd., into bankruptcy. The gentlemen admitted they had made a blunder by investing with the firm. The company claimed to be involved in the film industry and offered investment programs yielding 24% a year. I followed the investigation closely because one of the members of the firm had offered me referral fees for bringing in investors, and I had actually met with him at their lavish offices in Irvine. Because I felt intuitively uncomfortable there, I chose not to get involved, even when the individual, who is now in jail, called frequently to inform me that their investments were approved to be secured by the Federal government, minimum investment $10,000.

They had a compelling story, claiming that the founder of the firm was Sicilian, had ties in Sicily, owned a bank in Sicily, and could assist in off-shore banking and tax sheltering, i.e. evasion. Their investors included eminent sports figures, Hollywood stars, and high-flying corporate investors. Lured by the high yield, working people had moved their entire retirement funds into this company, often convinced by relatives whom they considered to be savvy investors.

When the court appointed an investigative team, they discovered that the officers of the firm had shared a jail cell, that the company was incorporated under the name of a chauffeur who didn't even know it, that the "Sicilian" had no old-world ties, and that apparently none of the money placed with them for investment had gone into investments, but rather had been spent to support luxuriously lavish life-styles for members of the firm: multi-million dollar homes, fleets of expensive cars, Nordstrom shopping, extravagant travel. The Sicilian was found dead in his mansion by apparent suicide during the investigation.

Fear and shame

The people interviewed by *Money* magazine claim to have learned from the mistakes, but admit the mistakes have made them fearful, less aggressive, less sure of themselves. Those duped by DFJ prefer not to be known. It is too humiliating. Their situation is beyond a "mere mistake." Fear walks hand in hand with shame. Guilt is something we may feel bad about inside for an error we made. The guilt we can own alone. Shame is public: "What will people say, what will people think?" It is hard to admit we made mistakes because we feel ashamed. If I were to ask you how many times you've arrived at your destination on time and without problems, you probably would be challenged to report. If I were to ask you how many times you've been lost and the circumstances, you could probably account for every one. If I were to ask you what you did "right" yesterday, you probably would be a while in putting together the inventory. If I were to ask you what you did "wrong," yesterday, what "mistakes" you made, you would have them right at the tip of your tongue, readily available in your conscious mind. You may have revisited those mistakes several times today already, and you may even have rehearsed how you might have altered and reversed the situation.

We can't learn less

When we put our energy into our errors, they are magnified out of proportion; and we then lack the energy to focus on the positive. We learn by trial and error. Mistakes are positive. The PBS special on Fuller's life shows the footage of the collapse of the first geodesic dome that he built at Black Mountain in North Carolina. One of his associates there that summer, who heard the great "whoosh" as it came tumbling down, said she felt heartbroken for him. But Fuller, undaunted, just observed that he never expected it to stay up, that he learned from seeing it fall down, that he learned through failure. Fuller tells us, "We cannot change one iota of yesterday." He also observes:

> ...Every time man makes a new experiment he always learns more. He cannot learn less. He may learn that what he thought was true was not true. By the elimination of a false premise, his basic capital wealth which is his given lifetime is disembarrassed of further preoccupation with considerations of how to employ a worthless time-consuming hypothesis...Every time we employ and test our intellectual know-how by experimental re-arrangement of physical energy interactions...we always learn more. The know-how can only increase.[8]

I urge you to use the following exercise to record and release the errors of the past. This will free you to be fully present in the present. Just as the roses under Emerson's window make no apologies, neither should you.

NO MISTAKES:

Only Opportunities to Discover

the Truth

Fuller notes: *"One of humanity's prime drives is to understand and be understood. All other living creatures are designed for highly specialized tasks. Man seems unique as the comprehensive comprehender and coordinator of local universe affairs."* Man comprehends through trial and error. Thus, we conclude: "There are no mistakes, only opportunities to discover the truth." This exercise is designed to assist you in re-framing your mistakes so that you begin to see them as opportunities. From each one you will be able to see that "you can't learn less" and your know-how can only increase.

Did you grow up thinking it was bad to make mistakes?

_____

_____

_____

_____

How were you punished for mistakes?

_____

_____

_____

_____

What do you say to yourself when you make a mistake?

_____

_____

_____

INVENTORY OF MISTAKES:

1.   List the worst mistakes you made over the past week:

_____

_____

_____

_____

What did you learn from each one?

_____

_____

_____

_____

Generalization: How did your know-how increase?

_____

_____

_____

INVENTORY OF MISTAKES:

1. List the worst mistakes you made over the past month:

_____

_____

_____

_____

What did you learn from each one?

_____

_____

_____

_____

Generalization: How did your know-how increase?

_____

_____

_____

_____

INVENTORY OF MISTAKES:

1. List the worst mistakes you made over the past year:

_____

_____

_____

_____

What did you learn from each one?

_____

_____

_____

_____

Generalization: How did your know-how increase?

_____

_____

_____

_____

_____

INVENTORY OF MISTAKES:

1.   List the worst mistakes you made over your lifetime:

_____

_____

_____

_____

_____

What did you learn from each one?

_____

_____

_____

_____

Generalization: How did your know-how increase?

_____

_____

_____

_____

In our society there is a standing antagonism between the conservative and the democratic classes; between those who have made their fortunes, and the young and the poor who have fortunes to make; between the interests of dead labor—that is, the labor of hands long ago still in the grave, which labor is now entombed in money stocks, or in land and buildings owned by idle capitalists—and the interests of living labor, which seeks to possess itself of land and buildings and money stocks.

Emerson, Napoleon; or, The Man of the World [1]

Leverage: More With Less

The ancient practice of usury

It used to be the practice in public schools for children to be required to memorize this passage from one of Shakespeare's best-known plays, *The Merchant of Venice*:

> The quality of mercy is not strained,
> It droppeth as the gentle rain from heaven
> Upon the place beneath. It is twice blest;
> It blesseth him that gives and him that takes.
> 'Tis mightiest in the mightiest. It becomes
> The throned monarch better than his crown.
> His scepter shows the force of temporal power,
> The attribute to awe and majesty
> Wherein doth sit the dread and fear of kings.
> But mercy is above this sceptered sway
> It is enthroned in the heart of kings,
> It is an attribute to God himself,
> And earthly power doth then show likest God's
> When mercy seasons justice.
>   Act IV, Sc. 1, ll. 184-197

It seems astonishing today that this speech is made as a plea to the Jew, Shylock, who has accepted a pound of flesh as the interest due from a Christian for borrowed money. In ancient times this practice was called *usury*, because the interest

187

charged is for the *use* of the money. Christians spurned this Jewish practice, considered it wrong. In the play, the borrower, Antonio, a Christian and a great pirate, loses his argosy from Tripoli at sea. His creditors swoop in on him, and he is declared bankrupt. This is Shylock's moment; he will have his revenge, his pound of flesh. A trial is called. Portia, in this famous speech, asks Shylock to show mercy. When Shylock refuses mercy, the tide turns against him. He may take the pound of flesh, "but not one drop of blood." Further, he, an alien, has sought to take the life of a citizen. For this he, Shylock, can die. The Duke resolves it by a pardon for Shylock's life, but grants Antonio half of all that Shylock possesses.

Interest: our usury-driven economy

Such a bitter confrontation over the charging of interest seems almost unfathomable today, so *usury*-driven is our economy. Indeed, the head of the Federal Reserve is watched more closely than the President of the United States, for he is far more powerful. He determines how much money will be available for ordinary citizens to use. The rate of interest charged for the use of money either curtails or accelerates our spending practice. It follows a policy we adopted at the end of the depression in the United States, a policy based on the ideas of the British economist, Maynard Keynes. When the unemployment rate goes down, the interest rate goes up. When the unemployment rate goes up, the interest rate goes down. The psychology of the marketplace is this: If more people are working and earning and spending, the economy risks inflation. To "cool" inflation worries, we must pay at the bank.

Maynard Keynes reasons that a man with money, like Shylock, has a choice. He can choose to lend his money for interest, or he can keep it liquid.

...we can usefully employ the ancient distinction between the use of money for the transaction of current business and its use as a store of wealth. As regards the first of these two uses, it is obvious that up to a point it is worthwhile to sacrifice a certain amount of interest for the convenience of liquidity. But, given that the rate of interest is never negative, why should anyone prefer to hold his wealth in a form which yields little or no interest to holding it in a form which yields interest...?[2]

Keynes continues with the choice between lending money for interest or investing it in capital assets:

The owner of wealth, who has been induced not to hold his wealth in the shape of hoarded money, still has two alternatives between which to choose. He can lend his money at the current rate of money-interest or he can purchase some kind of capital asset.[3]

The investment in capital assets is the other thing that makes the head of the Federal Reserve jumpy. If the wealthy man buys stocks, and the stock market is inflated, that is, the earnings of the company do not warrant the price of the stock, then the wealthy man may think he is wealthier than he is and take risks. He may borrow against what he has, buy more, and thus drive up the price of the stock even more. This is the situation now with the Internet stocks: earnings of the companies do no warrant the high price of the stocks. The head of the Federal Reserve sees this as an "inflation flag."

Interest and leverage

When we borrow money and pay interest for the use of the money, we are using *leverage*. The abundance of capital assets and the success of our economy is the result of effective use of leverage. All the wonderful things in our life that we take for granted, the factories that produce goods, the banks that circulate money and help us buy houses and start businesses, the schools and parks and concert halls and theaters, got here by leverage. The Christian distaste for the idea of paying interest, expressed by Antonio, denouncing it as unnatural and therefore immoral, had been generally replaced by Shylock's pragmatic viewpoint long before Maynard Keynes published *The General Theory of Employment, Interest and Money* in 1936. We accept the regulation of the rate of interest as a logical solution to economic problems and as the basis for our modern monetary system because we have no choice. Most of us don't even understand it. It's only important if we want to buy a house or a car, and we can't afford to pay cash.

Leverage: the physical principle

Why do we call it leverage? To visualize this, you may go back to your high school physics and remember that a lever is a mechanical device that allows you to lift up a large weight with a minimum of exertion. There is usually a fixed support, a fulcrum, upon which the lever rests. The lever is often a straight, flat device, rather like a crowbar. One end of the lever is on the fulcrum, and the other end of the lever is under the object to be lifted. The weight that one can lift with the lever far exceeds the weight one could lift alone. It allows the human being to do what would not be humanly possible.

The cave man's discovery

R. Buckminster Fuller hypothesizes that man's first experience with leverage came when a cave man walked across a woods, stepped on a tree lying under two or three other trees, and observed that stepping on the lower tree lifted a higher tree. Because it was not "humanly possible" to lift the tree, the cave man, Fuller imagines, probably thought it was magic and erected it as a totem pole. When he observed that any tree would do, and that it would happen over and over, he stumbled upon the generalized principle of leverage.

Metaphysical application of the physical principle

We have come a long way from the cave man's tree, the original lever, to the ATM. In so doing, we once again establish the unique ability of man to observe physical principles and to give those principles metaphysical application. Fuller describes this generalization of physical principle:

> Once man comprehended that any tree would serve as a lever his intellectual advantages accelerated. Man freed of special-case superstition by intellect has had his survival potentials multiplied millions fold. By virtue of the leverage principles in gears, pulleys, transistors, and so forth, it is literally possible to do more with less in a multitude of physio-chemical ways. Possibly it was this intellectual augmentation of humanity's survival and success through the metaphysical perception of generalized principles which may be objectively employed that Christ was trying to teach in the obscurely told story of the loaves and the fishes.[4]

Man's power of reason: observation, application, generalization

This is how man has mastered the physical universe. First he uses the physical principle, i.e. applies the lever to create gears, pulleys, transistors. He is able to do more with less exertion, to perform feats that are not humanly possible. As he observes the principle in action, he generalizes that principle, and then applies it somewhere else. That is the process of inductive reasoning: if this is true, and this is true, then this must be true. Man further masters the universe by taking the observed physical principles and applying them beyond the physical, metaphysically. We may have taken a rocket to the moon through the observation, application, and generalization of physical principles, but that is not how we *paid* for it. We paid for this endeavor and for the enormous improvement in our way of life here on the planet in comfort and services through the metaphysical application of the principle of leverage.

Bonds

Communities, states, nations, issue bonds for special projects: roads, bridges, parks, and rockets. Sometimes the specific purpose for a bond is stated; sometimes it isn't. For instance, a city may sell a municipal bond to pay for new schools. The citizens buy the bonds at a discounted price, for less than the face value stated on the bond. When the bond matures, they will be repaid what they have paid plus whatever rate of interest the bond yields. This is a win/win situation. The city treasury takes in an influx of money to pay for the project. This means that the schools can be built immediately. The city does not have to wait until enough money is collected in taxes or from a special assessment. The citizen purchasing the bond has the security of the municipality standing behind the bond and a predictable yield on a stated date as return on the investment. The community as a whole enjoys the benefit of good schools to attract people to the community.

U.S. Treasuries

Our U.S. Treasury sells bonds, bills, and notes. During World War II, we sold "war bonds." People bought these bonds to pay for the war effort. As children we could buy stamps that we pasted in a book. The stamps cost ten cents each. When the book was filled, we had eighteen dollars worth of stamps. We could trade the book in for a bond that would mature in twenty-five years and would be worth twenty-five dollars. This act of buying stamps and pasting them in a book probably had more value for the government psychologically than monetarily. We felt as if we were truly contributing to the war effort by saving our pennies.

Homes

When we buy a home, we use leverage in our purchase. Our lever is the down payment, the small percentage of the price that we pay at the time of purchase. The remainder of the purchase price, we borrow at a stated rate of interest. We can sometimes buy a home with a down payment of as little as five percent of the purchase price, lifting up ninety-five percent. Think what a difference this has made in the quality of life. If we had to wait until we had saved the full amount to buy a home, $250,000, how many people would own a home? If you drive south of Tijuana into Mexico, you see partially built and abandoned homes. They start out by laying a foundation, may put up a few walls, and then give up in discouragement. This is what happens without leverage for home purchase. Our mortgages provide us with instant gratification of the "American Dream."

The loaves and the fishes

Fuller says that the story about Jesus and the loaves and the fishes might have been Christ's way of teaching the metaphysical generalization of the physical principle of leverage. Let's explore the basis for that remark. In the story of the loaves and the fishes, Jesus is said to have fed a multitude with five loaves and two fishes. If you recall the story, Jesus had been with a multitude of 5000 people for an entire day. As evening approached, his disciples urged him to send the multitude away so that they could go to the villages to buy food.

But Jesus said unto them, They need not depart; give ye them
   to eat.

And they say unto him, We have here but five loaves, and two
   fishes.

He said, Bring them hither to me.

And he commanded the multitude to sit down on the
   grass and took the five loaves and the two fishes,
   and looking up to heaven, he blessed, and brake,
   and gave the loaves to his disciples, and the disciples to the multitude.

And they did all eat, and were filled: and they took up
   the fragments that remained twelve baskets full.

And they that had eaten were about five thousand
   men, besides women and children. Matthew: 16-21

Expectation, Belief, Word

In this account, as in the account of many of the activities of Jesus as documented by Matthew, Mark, Luke, and John, he demonstrates the power of the mind to determine the reality. This is true with his healings; this is true with his "miracles." This mental power is unlimited. Jesus' stories are all stories of Jesus taking the natural resources, wherever they are, be it a human body, a vessel of water, or the contents of a lunch bag, and transforming them by his *Expectation, Belief,* and *Word*. What is an *expectation*? "*Ex*" means out. *Spectare* means to look at, a derivation of *specere*, to see. So an expectation is just a looking out for, just as we look out for someone coming down the road. And what is a *belief*. Now "*bi*" means complete, "*lief*" goes back to Middle English "*bileafe*" and the Old English "*geleafa*," with a consistent meaning of acceptance of the truth of anything without certain proof; i.e. a mental conviction. We don't get too far in the dictionary with *word*: "A linguistic form that can meaningfully be spoken in isolation." You will recall that Fuller considers the *word* as the first industrial tool, i.e. a tool that is used by two or more. The first use of a symbolic sound as a means of communication became an industrial tool.

The power of the spoken word

Let us go back to the first chapter of Genesis to explore *word*. We are told this about the creation:

In the beginning God created the heaven and the earth.

And the earth was without form and void; and darkness
was upon the face of the deep. And the spirit of
God moved upon the face of the waters.

And God said, Let there be light: and there was Light.
Genesis: 1-3

As the act of creation is described, it has two parts: what God "says," his *word*, and what he "calls" what he has created i.e. "And God saw the light, that it was good: and God divided the light from the darkness. And God called the light Day, and the darkness he called Night." Nothing existed until God spoke it into existence, and it had no identity until God called it something, gave it a name. God had the *Expectation*, the *Belief*, and the *Word*. This is exactly the procedure Jesus follows as well. In Jesus' act of creation, or of <u>re</u>creation, as in turning water to wine or five loaves and two fishes into food for thousands, he acts upon the creative medium, whatever material he has before him with: 1) the *Expectation*; 2) the *Belief*, and 3) the *Word*. *Expectation*s, *Belief*s, and *Word*s are not packaged and sold at Wal-Mart. They are not available on the shelves of Home Depot. Grocers do not stock these items in the produce section or keep them in the freezer.

Free metaphysical commodities

Indeed, *these metaphysical commodities are totally free*. We can have as many of them, as much of them, as we choose. They are available to us every second of every minute of every hour of every day. They are without measurement, without quantification, without limit. All we need to create all we want is readily available to us all the time. We have only to *expect*, *believe*, and to *speak*, and it will be. We can do what God did; we can do what Jesus did. We do, in fact, unconsciously practice the same methodology every day; and we also accept the gifts of those who unconsciously utilize this methodology as a part of their daily business.

No restriction on your possibility

My intent, right here, right now, is to make you, the reader, conscious of this methodology so that you can draw on the unlimited ability of the universe to respond to your *Expectation*, *Belief*, and *Word* as effectively as both God and Jesus. This explanation corroborates the truth that nothing in the universe exists except thought and energy. That is the extraordinary message of leverage. Since God or Universe is the big thinker who thought it up, and since you uniquely have the ability to retrace the pattern of God's thinking, you have absolutely no restriction upon your possibility. We can create everything we need through *Expectation*, *Belief*, and *Word*, just as God does. This procedure demonstrates what man has already been able to create by generalizing upon an idea. This *idea*, something else we never find on the shelves of K-Mart and Target, originated in the physical image of the bottom tree lifting up the top tree. From it, we have produced a world of items, comforts, services, and agencies. The ingredients required to supply anything we want are totally free. This is what Jesus came here to teach us.

Promises and equivalents of exchange
Free promises

Man's culture evolved outward from his center, family to tribe to inter-tribal communication and exchange. Here we can embrace Fuller's image of the "great pirate" who had the courage to get into his canoe, travel from island to island, and discover the unique goods and services available there. This "great pirate" placed himself in the center, as the know-it-all of exchange, the ultimate power figure because he could get anybody anything. This early exchange was by barter. Man eventually observed that the barter system was cumbersome. After a while it got to be too much trouble to carry a cow to someone in exchange for fifty bushels of grain, so he invented a way to promise an equivalent, i.e. you owe me the worth of a cow in grain. Note that *promises are free.*

Promise of equivalence

When man began to dig in the earth, he came up with something shiny and scarce and for a long time, he tied the "promise of equivalence" to the metal he found in the ground: gold. This created more and better pirates, along with bankers, and thieves, considered in some circles as synonymous entities. But man, representative of the general population, didn't really care, so long as he could get his meat and potatoes. The precious nature of gold required variations in value, so for many centuries, man took other metals and used them as a medium of exchange, placing numerical values on "promises of equivalence," which worked so long as no one questioned the promise. Gold was always the bottom line, so we would say, to express this in words, that something was "as good as gold."

When man got to the point that he needed more "promises of equivalence" than he had gold, he did away with the gold and just issued the promise, a piece of paper that states, "In God we trust." A promise is expressed in words. In 1972, an American president, Richard Nixon, took the United States monetary system off the gold standard. We no longer required parity between the amount of gold we had on reserve and the number of promises we had issued, i.e. money. Maynard Keynes always considered the gold standard a "barbaric" practice anyway.

As good as gold

Women continued to go to the supermarket to buy groceries, men continued to go to the hardware store to buy trinkets to fix things, and car manufacturers continued to turn automobiles off the assembly line, all because we had been trained over the centuries to accept the promise because it was "as good as gold." And so it is. So long as man accepts the promise, it really doesn't matter exactly what is behind it. We don't even think to ask. We trust the system.

The American Dream
A home

The reason the United States of America has the highest standard of living in the world is because it has the most sophisticated way of using *Expectation, Belief,* and *Word.* We began in the 1940s to articulate the American dream: a house for every family, a chicken in every pot, and a car in every driveway. We made that idea a reality with another idea, a mortgage for the house, and a loan for the car, letting the bottom tree, a little itty bitty tree, lift up a great big tree. So to buy a house, we put a little bit down, and we go to the bank to get the rest. The bank takes our pieces of paper and our coins, issues a another piece of paper, a contract, on which words are written, and we sign the contract. Then we spend, theoretically, at least at the beginning, the rest of our lives, thirty years, paying back the bank. Bear in mind that it was very common for the American male to be dead at fifty or sixty when the American mortgage came into being. The average male in the 1960s would retire, pick up nine Social Security checks, and then die before 65.

A car

To buy a car we did the same thing we did to buy a house. We went to the bank and showed the bank that we had a little bit of money, i.e. currency, to put down on the purchase of a car. The bank took the currency and the car, pronounced them all the possession of the bank, and issued a contract, a piece of paper on which words are recorded. The bank then gave the manufacturer of the car a copy of the contract and a portion of the currency. The manufacturer then distributed currency to his employees, which they, in turn, took to the store to buy food for their families and took to the bank to buy houses and cars for themselves.

Ownership in the mind

An extraordinary thing takes place in the human mind when the coins, pieces of paper, and the words are thus exchanged, the promise of equivalence. The house, which actually belongs to the bank, in our minds becomes our house. We paint it, carpet it, landscape it, clean it, furnish it. We become citizens of our neighborhood. We go to the polls, and we vote to issue bonds for schools and parks and roads, because we are homeowners and we want our communities to be fine places to live. We take our car to the service station and change the oil. We wash the car, park it in the garage, and drive it carefully so as not to bang it up, because it is our car. The principle of ownership brings out the best in human nature, even though it may only be a combination of partial ownership and an idea based upon *Expectation*, *Belief*, and *Word*, a "promise of equivalence."

Fed funds: more promises

As the banks needed more and more paper and coins to empower Americans to have the idea of ownership, we created another idea. For every one piece of paper on deposit in the bank, assume $1 each, the federal government would let the bank have ten pieces of paper, $10. Initially, the federal government had as much gold on deposit as it issued in paper, the "promise of equivalence." When it needed more promises than it had gold, it kept the promise. It did not really matter so long as the government made the promise, and we accepted the promise.

Exchange based on promises and expectation

In fact, we have a world of exchange based on *promises* which are free. We act on *Expectation* of promises, as Keynes observed of the entrepreneur: "Meanwhile, the entrepreneur {including both the producer and the investor in this description} has to form the best expectations he can as to what the consumers will be prepared to pay when he is ready to supply them…after the elapse of what may be a lengthy period and he has no choice but to be guided by these expectations, if he is to produce at all by processes which occupy time."[5]

So long as we have the *Expectation*, the *Belief* and the *Word*, we really don't need anything else. As we shall see in the chapter on "True Wealth," this is how we went from being out of money to having enough money to wage World War I and World War II. Our system of free enterprise is an extension of both the metaphysical principle of leverage and the metaphysical practice exemplified by Jesus. Now it is the mission of the United States to teach the rest of the world to make the same

promises and to inspire the same application of *Expectation,
Belief,* and *Word* in their people. There is absolutely no limit to
what the mind of man can create out of the metaphysical. Jesus
did it. We do it. Actually, the only reality is the mind. The
mind is all there is. The only limitation you have upon you is
how you use your mind, how you direct and use your thoughts.

Leverage and daily practice

What can leverage mean for you in your daily practice, in
your business, in your work. It is always the principle of doing
more with less. The computer is a form of leverage. The program in the computer replicates the function of the human
brain. We could alphabetize all the listings in the telephone
book for the city of San Francisco by sorting them according
to the letters of the alphabet, and then within each letter, sorting and organizing. It might take us several months. The computer is programmed to do that for us. One program is
written; it is used by millions of people; each person using it
does more with less. That is why Bill Gates is so rich.
Computer software is a metaphysical lever. The Internet is the
next extension of that leverage.

Microsoft

The justice department of the U.S. Government has found
Microsoft to be a monopoly and wants to break it up. Why
should Time-Warner and AOL be allowed to merge, and
Microsoft broken up? This is political manipulation and punishment for success. Never in the history of man has leverage
been used so successfully to empower so many. This is
Microsoft's gift to humanity. Thousands of people have
become millionaires, and some have become billionaires both

because of the technology Microsoft has made available so reasonably and because of the example it has made for public offerings of technology stocks. The access to knowledge on the planet has been transformed by this use of leverage, with critical impact for all areas of life: home, business, schools, public institutions, government, private and religious institutions. No one has remained untouched.

Bill Gates assembles the brightest and best minds to solve problems and to create products that reflect those solutions. The public considers the intent of Microsoft and its leader to be benign. When I challenge young people to create the biggest picture they can for their lives, the computer whizzes want to work for Microsoft and to receive stock options. It used to be when a kid grew up, he wanted to be president. Today, he *and* she want to be Bill Gates. When I am at my computer, I feel as if Bill is by my side, my friend, sitting there with his impish grin. If I have a problem, I can call and get help or go on the Internet to find a solution. Bill Gates has done well for himself; he has done well for the planet.

Films, TV, radio

A single movie is produced, copies are distributed to theaters, and thousands of people can see it the first weekend. After the movie has completed its run in the theaters, it is recorded on video-tape, sold and rented, and millions of videos come into our homes. A live theater performance takes place only once. While a long run leverages the preparation of the actors, each performance is a separate event, subject to the elements that make live theater so unique an experience: the performance of each of the actors, the chemistry between the audience and the actors. Movies are frozen in time, permanent works of art. It is amazing to think that initially television was considered a threat to the film industry. Then the VCR was considered a threat. Television was supposed to do away with radio. Leverage actually augments opportunities. When we learn to do more with less, we create more avenues for participation and for consumption.

Books, CD's, t-shirts, posters, and prints

Every time you purchase a book, a CD, a print, a poster, or a logo t-shirt, you are consuming a leveraged product. I am using leverage right now. For eight years I have been teaching classes the contents of this book. Each class has a maximum of thirty-five students, and I teach usually three to five classes each year. This book can be printed and re-printed, and there is no limit to the number of copies that can be sold. The same is true when a musician does a performance. A single concert may be played for a thousand people. If it is recorded and sold as cassettes and CD's, then it can reach millions of people. A single t-shirt design can be replicated by silkscreen and printed on a million t-shirts. If an artist paints a beautiful picture in oils, then there is only one painting. If posters and prints of that painting are made, then the beauty of the painting can be enjoyed by millions.

Leverage opportunities limitless

You can think leverage. You can think about how you can take what you are doing, a single effort, and how you can replicate that. If you're engaged in work or a profession where you can't see an application for leverage, think about how you might modify your endeavors to employ leverage. When you conceive of yourself as self-employed, when you acknowledge that only thought and energy exist, then there is no limit to your possibility. The message of all great motivators is that there is no limit to the mind, to what we can achieve through our thought. That is the message of Napoleon Hill in *Think and Grow Rich*. As we have demonstrated here, that is the message of the greatest motivator of all, Jesus.

Use the following exercise to think about how you can employ the principle of leverage in your work, in your business, in your career.

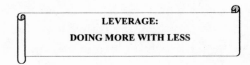

LEVERAGE:

DOING MORE WITH LESS

Fuller asserts: "Once man comprehended that any tree would serve as a lever his intellectual advantages accelerated. Man freed of special-case superstition by intellect has had his survival potentials multiplied millions fold. " We live in a culture that has maximized the concept of leverage metaphysically so that it has ever-increased our opportunity to "do more with less." Examine below the extent that you have capitalized upon leverage in your activities.

Places in my life where I use leverage now:

_____

_____

_____

_____

_____

_____

Leverage tools I take for granted, such as the computer and washing machine, are:

_____

_____

_____

_____

_____

_____

Tasks I presently perform where I could benefit from "doing more with less" are:

_____

_____

_____

_____

_____

_____

Leverage could affect my leisure activities if I used it effectively, for instance in making travel arrangements, etc:

_____

_____

_____

_____

_____

I could use leverage to increase my productivity at home, in my family, in my church in my community, and at work by:

Home:

_____

_____

_____

_____

_____

Family:
_____
_____
_____
_____
_____

Church:
_____
_____
_____
_____
_____

Community:
_____
_____
_____
_____
_____

Work: I could use leverage to increase my productivity by:

Hiring an Assistant:
_____
_____
_____

Creating a mailing?

_____
_____
_____
_____
_____
_____

Duplicating and marketing a creative product or activity?

_____
_____
_____
_____
_____
_____

I can make myself more consciously aware of opportunities to implement leverage in my activities by:

_____
_____
_____
_____
_____
_____

If I increased my productivity by 50%, I would feel:

_____
_____
_____
_____

This is how I would look:
In the picture you draw, include things such as home, car, recreation, family members, friends, status symbols important to you, hobbies, community involvement.

A man is like a bit of Labrador spar, which has no lustre as you turn it in your hand until you come to a particular angle; then it shows deep and beautiful colors. There is no adaptation or universal applicability in men, but each has his special talent, and the mastery of successful men consists in adroitly keeping themselves where and when that turn shall oftenest to be practised.

Emerson, Experience [1]

If our young men miscarry in their first enterprises, they lose all heart. If the young merchant fails, men say he is ruined. If the finest genius studies at one of our colleges and is not installed in an office within one year afterwards in the cities or suburbs of Boston or New York it seems to his friends and to himself that he is right in being disheartened and in complaining the rest of his life. A sturdy lad from New Hampshire or Vermont, who in turn tries all the professions, who teams it, farms it, peddles, keeps a school, preaches, edits a newspaper, goes to Congress, buys a township, and so forth, in successive years, and always like a cat falls on his feet, is worth a hundred of these city dolls. He walks abreast with his days and feels no shame in not 'studying a profession,' for he does not postpone his life, but lives already.

Emerson, Self Reliance [2]

Synergy

A typical office setting: Bartelby the Scrivener

Herman Melville's story "Bartelby the Scrivener: A story of Wall Street" is narrated by a lawyer who describes himself thus:

> I am a man who, from his youth upwards, has been filled with a profound conviction that the easiest way of life is the best. Hence, though I belong to a profession proverbially energetic and nervous, even to turbulence, at times, yet nothing of that sort have I ever suffered to invade my peace. I am one of the unambitious lawyers who never addresses a jury, or in any way draws down public applause; but, in the cool tranquility of a snug retreat, do a snug business among rich men's bonds, and mortgages, and title-deeds. All who know me, consider me an eminently safe man. The late John Jacob Astor, a personage little given to poetic enthusiasm had no hesitation in pronouncing my first grand point to be prudence; my next method. [3]

Turkey

This lawyer employs a staff of three in his office: Turkey, Nippers, and Ginger Nut. Turkey is named because of his face which glows red at the beginning of the workday, blazes by noon, and then settles to a burning coal by 6:00 p.m. He is a man about sixty years old, apt to be altogether too energetic, with a "strange, inflamed, flurried, flighty recklessness of activity about him." He is a good worker until lunch time; and then he falls apart, not only blotting the documents he copies in the afternoon, but also making a racket with his chair. He spills his sand-box, impatiently splits his pens "all to pieces" when he mends them, then in anger throws the pens on the floor "in a sudden passion" and leans over his table, "boxing his papers about in a most indecorous manner." He is rash, insolent, and subject to habitual temper tantrums. Although the lawyer prefers for Turkey not to work at all in the afternoon, Turkey insists upon it.

Nippers

These two older men in the office, the lawyer and Turkey, both "somewhere not far from sixty," are accompanied by two younger ones, Nippers and Ginger Nut. Nippers, a young man of 25, is the "victim of two evil powers–ambition and indigestion." He is definitely a candidate for ulcers: "The ambition was evinced by a certain impatience of the duties of a mere copyist, an unwarrantable usurpation of strictly professional affairs, such as the original drawing up of legal documents. The indigestion seemed betokened in an occasional nervous testiness and grinning irritability, causing the teeth to audibly grind together over mistakes committed in copying; unnecessary maledictions, hissed, rather than spoken."

Ginger Nut

Young Ginger Nut, a mere lad of 12, has been sent to the lawyer as an apprentice. He is a quick learner for whom "the whole noble science of the law was contained in a nut shell." Ginger Nut has earned his name by running a particular errand for Turkey and Nippers: "They sent Ginger Nut frequently for that peculiar cake–small, flat, round, and very spicy–after which he had been named by them." ("Ginger nut" is a British term; today, in the United States, we call the "ginger nut" a "ginger snap.") Turkey gets so carried away with eating Ginger Nuts in the afternoon that once he sealed a mortgage with one moistened between his lips.

Bartelby

When the lawyer receives a big contract requiring more copying than Turkey and Nippers are capable of performing, he hires Bartelby: "Pallidly neat, pitiably respectable, incurably forlorn." Bartelby works carefully, both day and night, "silently, palely, mechanically," and the lawyer would have been pleased with his diligence, had Bartelby been cheerful about it. But he was not cheerful about anything. Furthermore, Bartelby will not participate in the proofreading of his work. Whenever asked to do it, Bartelby replies, "I would prefer not to." Bartelby secretly takes up residence in the office, never leaving. Eventually, he, by his obstinacy, takes such control over the lawyer that the lawyer is forced to move his office elsewhere to get away from him.

Prefer not to

By the time they move, the word "prefer" has preferential status in all of their vocabularies, demonstrating Bartelby's profound influence. The new tenant can't move in because Bartelby is still there. When the old landlord, after pleas and threats, cannot get Bartelby to leave the premises, he asks the lawyer to intervene. The lawyer has no moral suasion whatsoever with Bartelby. The landlord calls the authorities, and finally Bartelby is carried off to prison where he "prefers not to" eat, and he dies. The lawyer describes him in his final fetal position: "Strangely huddled at the base of the wall, his knees drawn up, and lying on his side, his head touching the cold stones, I saw the wasted Bartelby."

Typical office dysfunction

This office drama may exaggerate what you have experienced, but perhaps not. We often find ourselves working at jobs where we blot in the afternoon, fuss and fidget, grind our teeth, hiss at our co-workers, have ambition to be the boss, run errands when instead we could be running the whole operation, and express "I would prefer not to," if not in words, then in deeds. Certainly, I have worked in many offices similarly dysfunctional; and I, too, have even performed dysfunctionally. When I think back upon it, the source of the dysfunction is a mismatch of temperament and skills with the assigned job.

The old man in the kitchen

It reminds me of the Swedish folk tale about the old man who worked in the forest, chopping wood and burning charcoal. He grew jealous of his old woman who merely sat at home cooking porridge, eating, and enjoying herself, or so he thought. The old woman, sick of his bickering, finally agreed to switch jobs. When the old woman returned from the forest with a big bundle of firewood on her back, she found her house in utter chaos: the dog had eaten the bacon; the bread had burned; the beer had run out of the barrel; the cream and the churn had fallen in the spring; her jacket was chopped for greens and cooked in the pot; the cow was hanged in the chimney; and the old man was burned and bruised. The old man discovered that domestic engineering requires multi-task capability, something women have naturally and men would probably "prefer not to." The old man cheerfully went back to the forest the next day.

Mismatched employment

Mismatching costs the employer and frustrates the employee. My first such experience occurred during the summer between completing my B.A. degree and starting work on my M.A. It was the first summer I hadn't gone home to work on my family's golf course. Through a friend I found a job as a typist at the Continuing Education Center of the School of Public Health. My boss, Ann Murphy, a quiet, orderly woman, a librarian by education, was in charge of coordinating conferences and then editing, printing, and disseminating the papers and speeches given in the conference meetings. To let you know how long ago this was, let me just say my pay was $2.25 an hour and the typing was done on typewriters without correction tape. A word processor or computer, if in existence, probably would have occupied a whole room. Correction tape, if invented, was not in common use, i.e. we didn't have any. Had there been "white out," it would have been forbidden.

At first Ann assigned me to type letters. She required that they be typed perfectly, without error. For the first two weeks, each day I went the whole day and never completed a single letter. Just as Turkey did, I blotted. I was afraid I'd get fired and not be able to pay my rent, and that just made my typing worse. Ann, the soul of resourcefulness and patience, not to have me undone by mechanical devices, hit upon another idea. She set me up with earphones to transcribe the tapes from the conferences. It didn't matter if I made mistakes in the transcription. Then after I transcribed the tapes, she let me rewrite the speeches and edit them for publication. Since I was an English major and enjoyed writing, this worked perfectly. I kept the job the whole year that I did my Master's degree, coming and going around my classes because my work didn't require a set schedule. She turned the letter typing over to the other two "girls" in the office, one a Chemistry major who always did everything perfectly, and the other, the mother of two small children who was absolutely meticulous. We were as snug as a bug in a rug. Our office was humming along synergistically.

Synergy common nomenclature

When R. Buckminster Fuller began to talk to university audiences about synergy in the 1960's and 70's, it was a new term. The book he wrote, *Synergetics*, appealed to his own specialized audience accustomed to unwinding the convolutions of his style and syntax. Here, forty years later, at the beginning of another century, "synergy" is common nomenclature. Stephen Covey makes it one of his "seven habits" of effective people in his book by that name: *The Seven Habits of Highly Effective People*. When I opened the Orange County South telephone book this morning and turned to the "syn" in the Business section, I found: Synergistic Electronic Systems, Synergistic Solutions, Synergy Computer Consultation, Synergy Electronics, Synergy Food Service Consultants, Synergy Staffing Inc, and Synergy Wellness Center. We thus see from this small sample the use of the term "synergy" in everything from electronics and computer networks to temp agencies and nutrition.

The toenail: no predictor

The early definition used by Fuller was that the behavior of wholes could not be predicted by the behavior of any one part, just as the toenail would not predict the whole body. When he made that analogy in 1963, he wasn't thinking about DNA.

Our nation had not yet suffered through the O.J. Simpson trial. Certainly a toenail does not look like the whole body. Further, it is appropriate, however, when presenting the concept of synergy that he would use the human body, for it operates according to cooperating and simultaneously functioning systems. Fundamental to Fuller's thought is his analysis of systems and his incredible respect for the geometrical, mathematical, overlapping, cooperating systemization of the universe.

The work of Deepak Chopra has made us even more sensitive to the perfection of the human system. Indeed, one might say that the systematic functioning of the human has become the paradigm for industry, for organizations, for marketing. When we are in perfect health, aware and accepting of ourselves, then we are functioning perfectly; and the chances are better for all that follows to function perfectly: the relationships, the family, the schools, the community, the nation, and the world.

Dysfunction: system awry

We have also come to a greater awareness that, unless we pay attention, we may spend most of our lives compensating in one way or another for the dysfunctionality of our parents, our families, our spouses, our social experiences, our work experiences. The word dysfunction assumes something in the system is awry, working improperly, one part throwing off the desired state, the perfect functioning of the system as a whole. To define and direct our experience, we must know why we think the way we do, why we accepted the attitudes and beliefs that affect our thinking. Only then can we understand how we got ourselves where we are. This gives us a choice: either to get out of the mess we're in or to make the best of it. Most of us assume we have only this voyage to set things straight. For those who believe we come back, the work of Brian L. Weiss, M.D., author of *Many Lives, Many Masters,* suggests we bring back what we failed to set in order, and it continues to upset the apple cart until we do.

A game of fortune?

We can effectively use the concept of synergy to address our choice, to figure out how to get out of the mess we're in or how to make the best of it. When we know the make-up of our particular cog in the wheel of fortune we have created for ourselves, we can love it or leave it. Fortune, *Fortuna,* usually bears the connotation of something good, or at least is conceived that way in our climate of opinion or our race consciousness. One goes off to make one's fortune. One plays the Wheel of Fortune to win prizes and a moment of glory. One buys lottery tickets. I actually sold a house to a woman who won the California lottery. In *Death of a Salesman,* Willie Loman's brother, Ben, headed for Alaska, was confused and turned around, and ended up in Africa, the Gold Coast. He tells Willie's sons, "Why, boys, when I was seventeen I walked into the jungle, and when I was twenty-one I walked out. And by God I was rich."

Thrown off!

A world-renowned astrologer, at least his fee supported the reputation that he was world-renowned, once did my chart. He said, "You have Jupiter in your first house. What this means is that Jupiter can take you up to the highest pinnacle, but he can also throw you off." Being "thrown off," unfortunately, is the other side of fortune. How many times have we all been "thrown off": thrown off in our health, thrown off in our job, thrown off in our relationships. We have a tendency when that happens to blame ourselves, and yet we very well may have been "thrown off" for a reason. Sometimes we have to be "thrown" to force us "to get back on our feet." Our folk language of old sayings certainly supports our experience. Sally Jesse Raphael has been a talk show host for seventeen years. She has been fired eighteen times.

Back on our feet

I have found the concept of synergy can serve us effectively as a way to come to understand ourselves so we can make wise decisions. No matter whom we wish to blame for the result, however we have turned out to be is the way we are. If we can accept and bless the result, then we have a chance to work with it effectively. If we fight it, then we will get "thrown off" in one way or another. There are a myriad of reasons we may not like the way we are: Mother expected better of me; I didn't pursue my father's profession; I'm not making enough money; I don't have enough education; I never got the opportunities my siblings did; just as I was about to make it, the economy or the market or real estate went all to hell. We have heard them all and used our excuse of choice. Actually, whatever happened is responsible for shaping you and making you who you are.

Quality functioning

My focus here on the concept of synergy will be personalized, directing our attention not on quality circles in an industrial setting, but on quality functioning at work, at home, and in life in general. The work of Richard Deming, rejected by our automobile makers at the end of World War II, was adopted by General MacArthur when he was charged with rebuilding Japan. Deming went there to teach the Japanese a method to involve the entire team contributing to the finished product in the design of the system to make and market that product, thus creating synergy.

The input of the worker on the assembly line was equally as important as that of the designer, the engineer and the director of marketing. It established an equalitarian acceptance of personal contribution and inspired a self-loving participation from each individual involved in the enterprise. Japan emerged with better cars than we were making in the U.S., and it sent our auto industry in the tank. We recovered our market share when we, too, adopted Deming's ideas and methodology.

Up close and personal: DISC

My personalized approach to synergy is meant to give you a similar sense of the importance of your special contribution and to inspire self-love. We will get up close and personal. The quality circles in all aspects of your life generate outward from your center. You know that center by knowing yourself. You are at peace and harmony with the person you are when you can bless and accept your part in the grand design. As we go through the following process, you have permission to let go of judgment of yourself, and to let go of judgment of others as well. The model I am using here is called the **DISC**,[4] and it is the basis of a psychological test used to build "high performance teams" or to determine aptitude for specific professions. It is a model that defines people by four factors, each of us tending to have a predominance in one of them, usually accompanied by at least a smattering of each of the four. The test determines the predominant factor by asking questions about preference, experience, and preferred solutions to challenges and situations. It is carefully constructed so that you can't outguess or manipulate your answers toward a preferred result.

Other psychological tests,[5] for instance the Briggs-Stratton, give similar information. My students resonate to the distinctions in the **DISC** test readily, and I suspect you may as well. Bear in mind as we go over these four personality types that we come in all sorts of mixtures, and harmonies, and balances. Yet each of us can probably find a predominance within one category and relate to it more specifically. Since the results of the test are placed on a graph, the predominant factor appears at the top of the graph and is therefore called "high." You will be "high" in one area and "low" or in the middle in the other areas.

D: Desire to direct and dominate other people. This personality type is egocentric, demanding, determined, driving, competitive, ambitious, creative, pioneering, opinionated, forceful, and decisive. The person who is high in **D** is likely to be an entrepreneur or to undertake whatever he does in an entrepreneurial manner. If he goes into real estate, he'll go with ReMax, a real estate firm made up of independent agents, rather than joining the Rock of Prudential, a firm with a strong corporate identity. He will create Apple in his garage. If he is a great teacher promoted to administration, he will go crazy in the bureaucracy and will either end up as president or out, i.e. thrown out. You don't need more than one high **D** at the head of a company, an organization, or a family. In fact, I once worked for a company headed by a husband and wife who were both high **D**'s. They spent every meeting arguing with each other, over-rode each other's decisions, and the company finally went under. It was embarrassing for employees to witness the exchange between them. I often wondered how confusing it must have been to their child.

I: Intuitive need to interact with other people. This personality type is warm, persuasive, optimistic, cheerful, caring, giving, empathetic, sympathetic, enthusiastic, and often political and jockeying for position, to the point of being effusive. If you go to a party with this personality, on the way home she will define each of the people she met with the statement, "He really liked me." The person high in **I** considers being liked as the most important thing in the world. She is likely to wear a necklace or bracelet or pin with her name on it. You knew her in high school because she would walk down the hall saying "Hi, how are you," to everyone, always running for Homecoming Queen. You may go to her with your problems because you know she cares. A high **I** may be good in sales, because you like her, but she'll need some high **D** as well to close. Never put a high **I** on an assembly line because she'll talk all the time and distract the other employees.

S: Takes pleasure in serving others. This person is a team player, result-oriented, dependable, takes direction well, reliable, patient, resistant to change, predictable, consistent, steady, stable, deliberate, passive. We rely on this person to open the store in the morning and to close it at night. We know that whatever we ask this person to do, he will do it. He never argues with you, never tries to outshine you, is willing to walk in your shadow and to make you feel important. The people high in **S** are needed in numbers by any effective organization, for they are the people who perform the tasks that need to be done to bring a product to market, to bring the goods for the bake sale, to keep the soccer team in clean uniforms and on the field. The high S's are the backbone of any enterprise.

C: Complies with the highest standards of excellence. This person is so self-critical and so self-demanding of accuracy that he is never finished with his research, never has quite completed his task, because he worries he may have missed something. He is intelligent, careful, cautious, indecisive, exacting, balanced, systematic, neat, and tactful. You know that this person will evade giving strong opinions because he will see both sides of the issue, will never quite complete his deliberation. You want this person in research, in accounting, in financial analysis and economic forecasting, in any area of an organization where a better solution may be found to a problem. It's important that the person high in C be able to stay in the background.

Each valuable

Each of these personality types and the various combinations of them contribute to the success of any enterprise. The most important issue is determining which personality type should be doing which task. You would not ask a person high in C to do public relations, or sales, or to act as the CEO of an organization. This personality wishes to be anonymous. You might place a person high in S in customer service, but only if it is balanced with I. You would not ask a high S to do telemarketing sales, especially out-bound, because she would freeze and never be able to pick up the telephone. You might place a high D in sales, in upper management, but you would never place him on an assembly line or in your research division. You would place your high **I** in human services, or sales, or public relations, but not in management or research. As a manager, being liked would take precedence over getting the job done.

Know yourself.

If you think back over your life, you may observe how often you have been misplaced or have been asked to do things contrary to your nature. I speak from my own experience. I didn't know that as a teacher I was an entrepreneur until I got promoted to administration, drove myself and everyone around me crazy, and then was thrown out. I was forced to explore fields that welcomed my personality type, *sales*: particularly stocks and bonds and real estate. If I were still an English Professor *a la* traditional *academia*, I wouldn't know how to write a contract, read a balance sheet, negotiate a deal or pick up a telephone to initiate a transaction. Although many academics place no value whatsoever on the skills I just mentioned, now so important to me, there may be an inkling of truth to the old saying, "Those who can do, do, and those who can't teach."

All part of whole

We carry with us from one time of life to another, from one work to another, all we have learned and all we have experienced. I approach my business as a teacher, counselor, listener, and closer. That's where a balance between the high **I** and high **D** for me is so crucial. The first time I took this test, I was off the chart as a high **D**. Now the two are balanced. It was the high **D** out of control that moved me to the next phase of my life.

Misplacement destructive

Although we can cultivate aspects of our personality that we wish to develop, it is important to avoid totally inappropriate work and relationship choices for our predominant personality type. Here is a flagrant and painful example of misplacement for a family I encountered in California. The father was a violinist and had held the equivalence to a tenured position in the Boston Symphony. His wife had held a research position with AT&T in Boston. When AT&T downsized, rather than giving her a golden handshake, she was transferred to California and placed in the sales division. Because they had two college-age children, and her income was higher, the husband gave up his position in the orchestra and followed her. When I met them they had one child at USC and one at Berkeley. The husband had been unable to find a position as a musician and felt dejected and depressed. He was doing telemarketing, hated it and hated himself.

Within six months the wife failed to meet her sales quotas and was terminated. AT&T must have known, should have known, that a research scientist would not succeed in sales. The research scientist, to be successful, is predominantly high in **C**, the opposite of the successful high **D**, high **I** sales personality. This family was cruelly disrupted and subjected to frustration and sorrow because of corporate decisions made without taking behavior factors into consideration. Or perhaps the corporation did take these factors into consideration and used this as a method to get rid of an employee with seniority without the cost of the "golden handshake." Had the wife in this instance a better understanding of her predominant personality type, she would not have accepted the sales job and would have looked elsewhere for a similar research position.

Correct balance effective

On the other hand, here is an example of a large pharmaceutical company taking advantage of sensitivity to personality types. This involves a brilliant young research scientist with a doctorate degree in Micro-Cellular-Developmental Biology, a definite high **C**. Before taking a position with a major chemical-pharmaceutical research company, he worked as a post-doctoral student at Stanford for three years, doing genetic research on myopia by studying *drosophila*, fruit flies. He is meticulous, careful, methodical. He is assigned to a team within the company designated to try out proposed solutions to specific problems to determine the feasibility of creating a new drug or a product to address the problem.

He complains that there is a woman assigned to his team who acts as a "tattle-tale," always reporting to the top management about their results before they are ready for anyone to know about them. This corporation has wisely and prudently placed a person high in **I** and **D** on this research team of people high in **C**. The **C**'s alone would never be finished, would never have results to share, because their research would never be quite done. This young man, incidentally, is married to a high **D**. They complement each other. In fact, in charting the results of the **DISC** test, a person high in both **D** and **C** has the "millionaire's curve," the ability to do the research and then take it to market.

Improve and understand relationships.

The **DISC** categories are not only useful for work experience, but also in personal relationships as, for instance, in the marriage mentioned above. People who stay married for fifty or sixty years usually complement each other rather than conflict. It is possible that two high **D**'s might be attracted to each other and might even stay with each other because of the challenge. Chances are, however, the need to be in charge will lead them to conflict. Here are two marriages.

The doctor and the High S

My father-in-law was a medical doctor and surgeon. He had tremendous high **D** at home and in the operating room and high **I** at the office when he interacted with patients. My mother-in-law was cheerful, with some high **I**, but she was predominately high **S**. She called my father-in-law "Doctor," ironed his socks as well as sheets and tablecloths on a mangle; and her pantry was perfectly ordered, with even each kind of soup carefully matched and stacked together. He was ill for several years before he died, and she lovingly nursed him.

My mother-in-law had always appeared to be strong and decisive. She always had opinions about issues and exercised leadership in her community. She and her husband had traveled together, building their trips around meetings of the International College of Surgeons. She had loved the travel, and I thought after his death she would travel again and recreate her life. On the contrary, it was as if she lost her identity when she lost him, and she became a recluse. She had identity as a doctor's wife, but not as an independent individual.

The farmer and his wife

My maternal grandmother, on the other hand, was a complete surprise to her family. She bore ten children, worked side by side with my grandfather in the farm fields, rode with him in the truck to market, waited on him "hand and foot," and took care of the house with whatever energy she had left, all high **S** activity. I saw her as a worn-out, overweight, farm-woman in a flowered house dress with run-down oxfords and varicose veins. When we were children, she would scare us if we were naughty by saying she would get her "dander up," and she would drop her false teeth; so I also considered her pretty mean and ugly, too. I can still visualize with horror her face with the dropping teeth by the light of a kerosene lantern.

When my grandfather died in his early sixties, my first discovery was the poetry and art and beauty in the soul of my grandmother. Her sister came for the funeral, and they recited poetry by memory for hour after hour. After the funeral, my grandmother dyed her hair back to its original auburn, bought new clothes, began to paint in watercolors and oils, learned to drive a car, and traveled around the country visiting her children and grandchildren. In retrospect, I see how much of her true personality, her high **I** she stuffed away and subordinated in her marriage to my very demanding High **D** German/Austrian grandfather who expected servitude from his wife and children.

The following exercise is designed for you to work with the basic type of personality you identify as your own, and then to inventory and analyze how much in harmony your work and personal relationships are. This should empower you to re-think and re-evaluate decisions you may have made or are in the process of making.

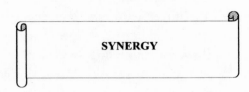

SYNERGY

Fuller defines synergy as the *"behavior of whole systems unpredicted by the separately observed behaviors of any of the system's separate parts or any subassembly of the system's parts."* My basic personality determines my behavior within any organizational structure and within any personal relationship.

Based on my understanding of the **DISC** model, I observe that I am predominately:

Personality: Type:

Because

_____

_____

My current work allows me to be myself because:

_____

_____

_____

_____

_____

My current work restricts my self-expression because:

Taking what I have learned about synergy into account, the operation of my workplace could be improved if:

My own productivity could be improved with these synergistic changes in my working environment:

The aspects of synergy I observe functioning effectively in my personal relationships are:

_____

_____

_____

_____

_____

Problems that could be addressed by taking synergy into account are:

_____

_____

_____

_____

_____

This that people say: 'Worship this god! Worship that god!—one god after anotherwhen speaking, 'voice'; when seeing, 'the eye'; when hearing, 'the ear'; when thinking, 'mind': these are but the names of his acts. Whoever worships one or another of these—knows not; for he is incomplete in one or another of these.

One should worship with the thought that he is one's self, for therein all these become one. This Self is the footprint of that All, for by it one knows the All—just as, verily, by following a footprint one finds cattle that have been lost...

Brihaderanyaka Upanishad 1.4.5 and 7 [1]

Character is this moral order seen through the medium of an individual nature. An individual is an encloser. Time and space, liberty and necessity, truth and thought are left at large no longer...He animates all he can, and he sees only what he animates. He encloses the world, as the patriot does his country, as a material basis for his character, and a theatre for action. A healthy soul stands united with the Just and the True, as the magnet arranges itself with the pole; so that he stands to all beholders like a transparent object betwixt them and the sun, and whoso journeys toward the sun, journeys towards that person. He is thus the medium of the highest influence to all who are not on the same level. Thus men of character are the conscience of the society to which they belong.

Emerson, Character [2]

Big Picture

To the Lighthouse: A Big Picture of achievement
If the weather is fine

The central issue in Virginia Woolf's *To the Lighthouse* is achievement, symbolized by reaching the Lighthouse. It becomes the "big picture" for several members of the Ramsay family and one of their guests, all assembled at the Ramsay's summer home at the shore in England. It begins with talk of the weather, "If it's fine tomorrow." The conflict in the plot is the life choice represented by the two parents, Mr. and Mrs. Ramsay. Mrs. Ramsay wants everything to stay just as it is, frozen in time, warm, comforting. Mr. Ramsay wants only the truth and will follow wherever it leads him. Mrs. Ramsay is soft and round, like a lap to sit in. Mr. Ramsay is hard and linear, like a remote Lighthouse on a rugged promontory. The son, James, is caught in the middle. James, only six, takes his mother's comment, "If it's fine tomorrow," as a promise that his dream of going to the Lighthouse will, indeed, be realized:

> To her son these words conveyed an extraordinary joy, as if it were settled, the expedition were bound to take place, and the wonder to which he had looked forward, for years and years it seemed, was, after a night's darkness and a day's sail, within touch. Since he belonged, even at the age of six, to that great clan which cannot keep this feeling separate from that, but must let future prospects, with their joys and sorrows, cloud

what is actually at hand since to such people even in earliest childhood any turn in the wheel of sensation has the power to crystallize and transfix the moment upon which its gloom or radiance rests...[3]

But: not fine

Then James' father, Mr. Ramsay, swoops down upon them and declares, "But it won't be fine." There it is, that *but*, the most powerful word in the English language: "Had there been an axe handy, or a poker, any weapon that would have gashed a hole in his father's breast and killed him, there and then, James would have seized it. Such were the extremes of emotion that Mr. Ramsay excited in his children's breasts by his mere presence."[4] James is caught between his intuitive, loving, ingratiating, exaggerating mother, who wants everyone to be comfortable and cozy and harmonious and hopeful; and his ramrod father, truth telling, domineering, stern: "He was incapable of untruth; never tampered with a fact; never altered a disagreeable word to suit the pleasure or convenience of any mortal being, least of all of his own children..." [5]

Caught in the middle: the dilemma

To stay with the known, the warm and cozy, or to go with the unknown, to be tested, that is the question, the dilemma. The entire household, the eight Ramsay children, the houseguests, all are immobilized, caught between the comfort of Mrs. Ramsay's beauty and charm and the cold, hard, bright light of truth represented by Mr. Ramsay and by the Lighthouse. Mr. Ramsay, a philosopher, attempting to put all thought in order A to Z, has never been able to get beyond

"Q" in his thinking. One guest in particular, Lily Briscoe, a maiden lady, is painting a picture which she can't get quite right. What holds her back? Her painting is an act of *self-assertion*, a frightening thing, against all that is honored in the present "climate of opinion." Charles Tansley, another houseguest, taunts her by muttering, "Women can't paint, women can't write." As for Mrs. Ramsay, Lily can only acknowledge the awful truth parenthetically, "(but Mrs. Ramsay cared not a fig for her painting)".[6] Lily is paralyzed by her own thinking.

Mrs. Ramsay: the comfort of the status quo

Mrs. Ramsay is a potent force on everyone's thinking; for she dominates and determines the climate of opinion. Mrs. Ramsay, who never wants her children to grow up, who knows they will "never be so happy again," dislikes the things said about her, "wishing to dominate, wishing to interfere, making people do what she wished–that was the charge against her and she thought it most unjust." It's just that when she looks at life, "a sort of transaction went on between them, in which she was on one side, and life was on another, and she was always trying to get the better of it, as it was of her…for that reason, knowing what was before them–love and ambition and being wretched alone in dreary places–she had often the feeling, 'Why must they grow up and lose it all?'"[7]

Mr. Ramsay: The Lighthouse a stark tower of truth

Mrs. Ramsay dies, the house is left alone for years; she is a memory. Then the family returns, the children now teenagers. Lily Briscoe is with them. The family is going to the Lighthouse. The day they go—Mr. Ramsay, his son James, and his daughter Cam—Lily stays behind. She finds in the house the old picture, takes up her abandoned work of art, and begins once again to paint. The children in the boat, now grown, observe their father, re-live their emotional battles with him, James re-envisioning the knife with which he wanted to stab him. He observes his father "getting his head now against the Lighthouse, now against the waste of waters running away into the open, like some old stone lying on the sand; he looked as if he had become physically what was always at the back of both of their minds—that loneliness which was for both of them the truth about things."[8]

Then they reach the Lighthouse: "So it was like that, James thought, the Lighthouse one had seen across the bay all these years; it was a stark tower on a bare rock. It satisfied him. It confirmed some obscure feeling of his about his own character."[9] Mr. Ramsay, who never praises James, says to him of his steering, "Well done!" At this moment of arrival, Lily finishes her picture: "With a sudden intensity, as if she saw it clear for a second she drew a line there in the centre. It was done; it was finished. Yes, she thought, laying down her brush in extreme fatigue, I have had my vision."[10] Only after Mrs. Ramsay is dead can this family go to the Lighthouse, can Mr. Ramsay begin to get beyond "Q," and can Lily finish her picture. They achieve the "big picture" conceived in their minds more than a decade earlier.

Confront the canvas the universe provides.

The family in *To the Lighthouse* is Virginia Woolf's family; the mother is her mother; the setting is their summer home. She adored her beautiful, albeit narcissistic mother; yet it was from her stern father, Leslie Stephen, that she took in the true grit required to be a writer. *To the Lighthouse* is Virginia Woolf's greatest literary achievement, and my brief summation here does not begin to do justice to her artistry as a writer. Our subject, however, is "the big picture," that is, the boundary that we all create around the vision for our life.

Every "big picture" is born into a climate of opinion. Many years ago I wrote a doctoral dissertation on Virginia Woolf's fiction and Post-Impressionist painting. As I look back upon my choice of subject matter, I realize that I related at a subconscious level with being pulled apart between two parents similar to the Ramsays, caught in their sentence upon my life. That moment of triumph, when Lily finishes her picture, symbolizes the necessity to leave behind the messages from the past and to confront the canvas the universe provides for us, to make our own mark upon life and upon our destiny. It requires a vision, and it requires the courage to set a navigation path to reach the Lighthouse.

How big can we think?

Fuller observes, "If it is true that the bigger the thinking becomes the more lastingly effective it is, we must ask, 'How big can we think?' "[11] When Moses was led by the Lord up onto the mountain top, he was told that all the land he could envision, his feet could trod upon. It sounds simplistic to say that we can only be as big as we can think, but it is true. The circumference around our life is determined by our expectation, and our expectation is a reflection of our thought. Recall Jesus, the *Expectation*, the *Belief*, and the *Word*. "Expectation" is the first step to realization. Fuller cautions, "But if we don't really know how big 'big' is, we may not start big enough, and are thus likely to leave unknown, but critical, variables outside the system which will continue to plague us."[12] Napoleon Hill tells us in *Think and Grow Rich*, "What the mind can conceive, it can achieve." Has anyone ever achieved more than his mind could conceive? Someone may tell us the good things that happened were "beyond my wildest dreams." Probably not!

Three big D's: Devotion, Dedication, Discipline

The dreams are wild because they are so "out there." We may even be afraid to have them in public, as Emily Dickinson says, "so public like a frog." When we make a public avowal, we make a spoken commitment. John F. Kennedy made a public avowal of a wild dream: putting a man on the moon. Once it was spoken, it became a possibility: *Expectation, Belief, Word.* He used the first industrial tool, the spoken word, to forge a commitment to a wild dream. When the "Big Picture" goes public, the forces marshal three big D's to make dreams reality: Devotion, Dedication, and Discipline. Without these, great ideas slip away into the residue of the little d's: down the drain of discarded dreams. Books have been written about the conception and achievement of the "big picture" of Henry Ford and Thomas Edison, of other great thinkers and doers. I have chosen here to bring this down to a homely level, to a story in which I have personal involvement. We often feel intimidated because it seems as if one man does it alone. The truth is Henry Ford's "big picture" could not be realized without the efforts of the Ford Motor Company; John Kennedy's "big picture" could not be realized without NASA.

Down to earth

The life story, the lifeline, in my father's family effectively illustrates the necessity that the "big picture" be publicly declared and collectively adopted for it to be realized and achieved. The word must be spoken to mobilize the resources.

Then the individual's commitment to the three big D's: Devotion, Dedication and Discipline have a medium in which to unfold, even when the prevailing climate of opinion, filled with doubts and hesitation, fails to nurture and support the "big picture." I have chosen this story as an illustration because it is closer to home for most of us who do not foresee becoming a Ford or an Edison.

Two homely examples
A big picture gone awry

My father was in the middle of twelve children born to a wiry and intelligent Ohio farmer and a woman from an Illinois family whose members were notable for their large, tall frames, and a set of the jaw known as "Jim jaw." This was a common designation where I come from. I'm not sure exactly who "Jim" was originally, but I know that all of my great aunts and great uncles on my grandmother's side had it. It is a set of the jaw, slightly protruding, firm, unmoving, symbolic of steadfast determination. If the determination were in your favor, you would be flushed with confidence. If the determination were against you, you felt like a whipped dog, actually victimized by the set of the jaw of the one who is an antagonist to any project or idea, especially yours.

Dead set Jim jaw

My grandmother's "Jim jaw" was dead set against my grandfather. He gave up his farm in Ohio, moved to southern Michigan, and bought a coal yard. As the story goes, he put the coal yard on the line for a section of land in the Upper Peninsula of Michigan. A section, you will recall, is big, 640 acres. The Upper Peninsula is rugged, with a long, dark winter, a short summer and growing season, still, even today, relatively desolate, predominantly wooded timber and iron country. The Detroit automakers used to take their enemies up to the corporate "hideaway" for deer hunting and bump them off, by accident, the first day of deer season. Perhaps they still do. Who would know the difference?

The people who settled in this remote place came from Sweden and Norway. It reminded them of home. Since I spent twenty-five years with my former husband's family driving back and forth to a cabin in the Upper Peninsula, 500 miles each way, to a spot on a lake that for many of those years had only a rude cabin with a pump and an outhouse, I can appreciate my grandmother's point of view. She was a sitter, not a doer; a bystander, not an innovator; a user of goods, not a maker; a receiver, not an initiator. There is a saying in the Midwest, "Aunt Mame sits broad." My grandmother's name was Flora May, and she sat broad. I loved her to pieces as my grandmother with the welcome lap. She was a Mrs. Ramsay. Had I been my grandfather, I wouldn't have chosen her as my "helpmate."

Desperate: out of hope

My grandfather's name was Edward Wood, and I suspect a part of him felt chained to "dead wood" when it came to his dreams and his vision. He wanted to relocate and start a new life. That was his "big picture." My grandmother refused to go. The idea of cultivating that 640 acres of forest and farm land was my grandfather's "big picture," but my grandmother did not buy into it. The lips closed firmly, the jaw went "Jim," and the issue was deadened in hostile silence.

My grandfather deserted. He just flat ran away and left my grandmother with that whole houseful of kids, ten of them.

Twice he returned, and twice my grandmother was pregnant again. All my childhood I was told that my grandfather was a despicable man, today's dead beat dad. Soon after I married, my first summer at that remote cabin in the Upper Peninsula, my Aunt Cora, the oldest child and the family organizer, came to visit. The setting must have taken her back to her own childhood. She said that there are always two sides to a story. When my grandmother effectively demolished my grandfather's dream, he ran away.

Telling faces

Since as a child I studied faces, the face of my mother, my father, my grandmother, my aunts, my uncles, always looking for signs of assent and for signs of negation, I felt a connection at that moment with this frustrated, desperate man. He was out of hope. That's what the word *desperate* means. My grandmother was my primary care-giver in her home from the time I was six months old until I was five. Then she came to live with us from when I was seven until eleven. I knew her face well. I knew when I was a good girl, and I knew when I overstepped my bounds. Grandma's punishment suited her nature, psychological, not physical. She made me sit on a chair or stand in a corner. I cracked the wallpaper in every corner of the house. That was the only way you could get back at that "Jim jaw," to crack the wallpaper.

Sex and family: a perceived trap

When Grandma Wood finally had her own house again, a little tiny house on Division Street, I would go and spend the night with her, mow her lawn, take down the screens and put up the storm windows. She was a large woman, almost 5'9", with ample flesh. She wore a tight corset, and I can still smell the scent when she let loose the ties and the corset slipped down to her ankles, over the loose, billowy underpants that she wore under it. It was mysterious, and I remember that it provoked from me the question about why she took my grandfather back when he returned, creating Clara, who died in childhood, and Uncle Walter, the youngest son. She said that someday I would be a woman and I would understand. Now I am a woman, and I do understand that glimmer of hope her sexual attraction would bring her husband back to her. I can also understand the grandfather who must have felt sexuality trapped him into the web of a spider, one who only wanted to sit and spin, who dominated the whole territory, and who left no space for his self-expression. His big picture was sucked into the web like a fleeting fly devoured in a trap.

Dismal Great Depression

Whatever my grandfather's feelings may have been about the destruction of his dreams, he was irresponsible to his wife and his children and wreaked great hardship upon them. During those depression years, there was scarcely enough to eat; and they survived by the charity of Mr. Cohn who owned the corner grocery store and "ran a bill" for the family. Grandma made milk gravy; the children took turns eating meat. The oldest son, Chester, worked at the cigar store and brought his entire pay every week home to his mother to care for the family. It was said he had a girlfriend, but we never met her; and his life was placed on hold for his mother and brothers and sisters. He died at forty, before he ever had a chance to have a life of his own. Since I stayed with my grandmother during the day while my parents worked, I remember running to meet Uncle Chester every Friday afternoon when he got his paycheck. He always stopped at Mr. Cohn's to get me a vanilla ice cream cone. That's when vanilla was pure, and the ice cream was made with real cream, and nothing ever tasted so good.

A big picture realized

One might say the dashing of my grandfather's "big picture" created the climate of opinion in which my father's "big picture" could be sparked and ignited. All of the twelve children worked; and my father, from the age of ten, was a caddy at the Lenawee County County Club. During the summer he would spend the nights there, sleeping outside, because it was too far to ride his bicycle home. He developed an early love of golf which he retained until his death. The men who hired him as their caddy were the most wealthy citizens in the county, and he also came to hold the vision of himself with a large wad of bills in his pocket, readily able to pay for anything.

His name was LeRoy, in French meaning "the king: *Le Roi.* He was a Leo. Since he was very bright, he skipped grades in school, and graduated at 15. He always regretted that, because he felt he wasn't mature enough to make good decisions. He took a job at the Simplex Paper Corporation in Adrian, Michigan at the age of 15, and entered a life as a factory worker, first doing drafting, then eventually being promoted into management, overseeing the shipping: traffic manager. He married my mother when he was 22 and she was 21.

Breaking free from the shackles

My mother was aggressive, a first child, very tough and resilient. She was named Delores, derived from the Italian, a river of grief, *Doloros.* Her brothers and sisters called her

"Dodie." She grew up on a farm, the daughter of an Austrian/ German father who had ten children who were expected to work for him. His will was powerful, and my mother's escape was not easy. Her aunt sent her and her sister, Virginia, to a Seventh Day Adventist nursing school after graduation from high school. They received constant letters from their father to come home and help with the farm. This made the girls feel guilty. Further, they were driven to homesickness by the Seventh Day Adventist prohibition of eating meat. They grew up butchering cows and hogs, making sausage, always eating heartily, even though there was little spare money. When they got busted for having canned sardines hidden under the mattress, they gave up and went home.

Under the gun

Mother and Virginia got away from the farm by moving into town and working at the American Chain and Cable where Mother was a time-keeper. She met my father when she was 21 and he was 22. They married soon after. When I was born in 1938, no one wanted a baby. The United States was still depressed economically, and war had begun in Europe. They were dark days, filled with uncertainty. My whole childhood was spent with relatives who were factory workers and union members. My mother had come to value the union soon after she went to the American Chain and Cable. She was such a hard worker, she out-performed everyone else. Then, one day, when she didn't feel well, she was pushed and penalized for poor performance; and she recognized the need for worker protection.

The factory: chained

The factory was the life source for my father's family. My uncles all worked in a factory or foundry. I think it is fair to say that my father was the most intelligent male in the family, only matched by my Aunt Cora who, were she born later, would have run a town or a company or even a country the way she ran her twelve siblings and her church. The Simplex Paper Corporation, the factory where my father worked, in my mother's mind became the place where my father would be chained and rot; his staying there to her symbolized lack of initiative and drive. When they fought, and they fought frequently and violently, all my childhood, she would say to him, "You're just yellow, and you'll never get out of that Simplex." My father's early childhood experiences made security very important for him, and he was fearful to let go of stability.

The union and the corporation

The company, the Simplex, noted in my father the same thing my mother did, the inner resources and ability to be more and do more. My father displayed his leadership ability quickly, and when he was in his late 20s, held an executive position in the Michigan CIO labor union. It was soon after a big convention in Grand Rapids, Michigan where my father was elected to an office, that the company promoted him. They probably feared his power as a potential troublemaker and moved him into management to get him out of the union. I was only five years old at the time and do not recall the conversations about the promotion, but I suspect that he was lured by the increase in money and the control over his time. For whatever reason, the navigation path he chose then was crucial, because it opened a new horizon for his thinking.

The entrepreneurial spirit

My parents were entrepreneurs in their hearts, but neither was capable without the other. My father had the mind, the thought, the plan. He was a high **C** with almost equal high **D**. My mother, a high **I**, had communication and a power of execution. As a farm girl, she didn't mind hard work, long hours, doing whatever it took to get a job done, even the most menial of **S**-type tasks. Together they were a synergetic union. Once my father was in management, he could take phone calls at work and come and go more freely. He and my mother accepted an invitation from my Uncle Bill and Aunt Connie, who had a successful clothing business in nearby Blissfield, to go into a clothing business with them in downtown Adrian.

Mother left the factory to work full-time in the store. It was a glorious place for her. She expressed her flair for fashion by buying for the store. She was always at least two years ahead in her ability to pick styles and colors, and at 84 is still always a "fashion plate." Her great people personality emerged in her interaction with the customers, and she brought warmth and sparkle to the endeavor. My father, who was meticulous in everything he did, discovered a talent for measuring men for tailored suits, and soon they had a flourishing business. Uncle Bill and Aunt Connie seldom came in the store.

The vision

Some personal life changes, apparent reversals, again moved my father closer to his "big picture." My mother became pregnant with my middle sister, Patricia. She had had several miscarriages, and the doctor told her she would have to have complete rest to carry this baby to full term. My parents sold out their half of the store to my aunt and uncle. Without my parents, the store went under; and my aunt and uncle never spoke to any of us again. As a store owner, however, my father had become active in the Jr. Chamber of Commerce; and given his natural leadership ability, he was elected president. One of the projects of the JC's was to draft a plan for a municipal golf course. With his love of golf, he had worked on the project and was an ardent advocate. The City, however, turned down the idea as too costly for such a small community, at that time around 18,000 people. One summer, when I was fifteen, my father took my mother out for her first game of golf. She had a wonderful time; and when he told her that he had always dreamed of building a golf course, she said, "Let's do it."

The execution

My father had the idea and the executive decision-making; my mother had the personality to attract a clientele and the willingness to do whatever it took to get the job done, whether that meant mowing fairways or cleaning the pro-shop. Unlike my father's parents before him, my parents had the right combination to succeed, together. They had the three D's to realize their big picture: Devotion, Dedication and Discipline. Public avowal, however, was painful. My parents bought a 65-acre cow pasture and began to build this "golf course."

It's very much like a *Field of Dreams*: build a place and they will come. The first year my grandfather came and planted a crop of rye to give the grass a foundation. Since all of my parents' saved resources went into the purchase of the land, the process of building this golf course was totally hands-on. My father continued his job at the Simplex and came after a full day's work to work for himself. The greens were hand built with a shovel and a rake. We planted the Seaside Bent grass seed; and as the seedlings began to sprout, my mother and I weeded the grass on our hands and knees. My father laid out the course. The first three years you couldn't tell the rough from the fairway. It was all rough.

The navigation path

In the middle of this enterprise, my father had his appendix removed; and when the doctor went in, he discovered abdominal adhesions from the year my father spent in his twenties, bedfast in a sanitarium with tuberculosis. The doctor went out of town immediately after the surgery, my father developed peritonitis, and almost died. When he went into the hospital, he weighed 220 pounds; he emerged from the hospital at 135. He was essentially an invalid, unable to work at his job or to help with the golf course. This left my mother and me. We had no income. My grandfather overheard a conversation about the "fool in Adrian who was losing his shirt," and he came to the rescue by directing my uncle, who owed my grandfather money, to pay my parents, instead. Each Friday my uncle Melvin would come and give my mother a payment. One other uncle came to our aid, my Uncle Archie who also worked at the Simplex. He would come out after work and help my mother with the mowing.

A year too early

Out of financial necessity, we opened the golf course a year too early. It was, indeed, a rough play. The barn on the property became our pro shop, right where the cow stalls had been. Later we even sold the house in town and moved into the upstairs of that barn. At first we had no rest rooms, only a chemical toilet upstairs in the loft where the hay had been kept. We had no sprinkler system. I would get up a 4:00 a.m.

and begin my day watering greens. Our clientele came mostly over the border from Ohio, and we were bitterly assaulted with jeers from the first players because the course was not ready.

The reasons for complaint were manifold. The people in Adrian were so resentful of my parents' steadfastness to their dream that many refused to come out and play on the course. Initiative provokes envy. Even our relatives jeered at us. Aunt Cora would come out and park her car across the road, and from there she expressed her resentment that my parents were so busy working they never had time to "chew the fat." This is where the "Devotion, Dedication, and Discipline" became so essential. We stuck to it. Work was all we knew.

A realization at great cost

My father got better. He began to collect the money from cart rental as a roll of $1 bills to be used for tree money. Until his death, he had that roll of bills in his pocket. My parents planted trees. They acquired more land, an adjacent orchard. They built another nine holes. When they finally sold the golf course to retire to Florida, it was one of the finest eighteen-hole public courses in southern Michigan. They had realized their big picture.

Expectation, Belief, and Word in action

What are the lessons we can draw from this? *Expectation*, *Belief*, and *Word*:

1) The mental "big picture," *Expectation*, is essential to successful creation.

2) Collective adoption of the "big picture," *Belief*, marshals the resources to bring the "wild dream" into reality.

3) Public avowal, the *Word*, is an important part of the commitment process. When you speak your *Word*, you bring the idea into focus; you plant the seed and express your intent to nurture it and to make it grow.

4) The 3 D's, Devotion, Dedication, and Discipline, make it happen.

5) The big picture must be broken down into manageable, reachable, measurable goals.

6) A navigation path must be set, each goal reached becoming a stepping-stone to the next.

Chunked down and accomplished

Note within this process that each step was an individual goal to be chunked down and then accomplished: The acquisition of the land, the rye grass base, the lay out of the course, the assembly of the basic tools and machinery, the building of the greens and the tees, the transformation of a cow barn into a pro shop, the stocking of the retail store. Each step had to be achieved to put it all together. Note each element has within it a measurable goal, a point at which achievement can be determined. Had I known then what I know now about real estate, we would have added another step and built houses around the periphery, becoming one of the first golf course developers.

Navigation: dismissing macrocosmic and microcosmic irrelevancies

The best thing about a navigation path is that it can be changed. Storms do come up unexpectedly. My parents never expected my father's prolonged illness. You can go at the same goal with the same big picture in mind from a different direction or with a different timetable. When you have a navigation path, you are the captain of your ship, you are the maker of your fate. Use the following exercise to create your own big picture. Make it as big as you can possibly imagine, for it is only your thought that limits. Remember, only energy and thought exist. Just as you can control your navigation path, you can control your thinking. As Fuller tells us, "Thinking itself consists of self-disciplined dismissal of both the macro-cosmic and microcosmic irrelevancies which leaves only the lucidly-relevant considerations."[13] When you conceive your big picture, consider fear of failure and fear of inadequacy as "irrelevancies." Any previous limits you have set for yourself are "irrelevancies."

BIG PICTURE AND
NAVIGATION PATH

Fuller queries: ***"If it is true that the bigger the thinking becomes the more lastingly effective it is, we must ask, 'How big can we think?'"*** How big can you think? Since the only restriction placed upon your big picture is your imagination and belief, make the picture below as big as you can. As Fuller cautions, "…if we don't really know how big *big* is, we may not start big enough." Be generous!

Draw a picture of you when your "big picture" is achieved. What will you be doing? What will you be wearing? Where will you be doing it? Who will be in your sphere of influence? How will you feel about yourself? Think of this as a cartoon someone might do of you when you are important enough to be noticed. A caricature always stresses the strongest and most salient features.

Now state this "Big Picture" in words. Be sure to use your name.
My "Big Picture" for my life is:

To set my navigation path, here are seven things I need to accomplish, listed in order of priority. For each achievement, I have a measurable goal with a specific timeframe; and I employ leverage and synergy. Seven is the number of completion.

1:

Goal:

2: _____

_____

Goal: _____

_____

_____

_____

3: _____

_____

Goal: _____

_____

_____

_____

4: _____

_____

Goal: _____

_____

_____

_____

5: _____

_____

Goal: _____

_____

_____

_____

6: _____

_____

Goal: _____

_____

_____

7: _____

_____

Goal: _____

_____

_____

Babylon is an outstanding example of man's ability to achieve great objectives, using whatever means are at his disposal. All of the resources supporting this large city were man-developed. All of it riches were man-made.

George, S. Clason, The Richest Man in Babylon[1]

Wealth has its source in applications of the mind to nature, from the rudest strokes of spade and axe up to the last secrets of art. Intimate ties subsist between thought and all production; because a better order is equivalent to vast amounts of brute labor.

Emerson, Wealth [2]

All is waste and worthless, till
Arrives the wise selecting will,
And, out of slime and chaos, Wit
Draws the threads of fair and fit.
Then temples rose, and towns, and marts,
The shop of toil, the hall of arts.

Emerson, Wealth[3]

True Wealth

a tiny amount, part or piece

Not one iota of yesterday

When Fuller discusses and defines wealth, he describes a scene, similar to the sinking of the ship in *Titanic*, to demonstrate that we "cannot change one iota of yesterday." A billionaire and his wife have gone on board a ship. He has brought along his stocks, bonds, deeds to property, diamonds, gold bullion, and his checkbooks. When the ship goes down, none of this material wealth can save him:

> So I would say he hadn't much left either of now or tomorrow in which to articulate his wealth, and since wealth cannot work backwardly his kind of wealth is vitally powerless. It is really a worthless pile of chips of an arbitrary game which we are playing and does not correspond to the accounting processes of our real universe's evolutionary transactions. Obviously the catastrophied billionaire's kind of wealth has no control over either yesterday, now, or tomorrow.[4]

Not measured in goods

Fuller is demonstrating that true wealth is not derived from pieces of paper, hunks of metal, stones, sovereignty-acquired interests in land, or theoretical ownership of enterprises. The wealth measured in gold, diamonds, currency, real estate deeds of trusts, stocks and bonds can be lost, can be taken away. It is all an arbitrary measurement created by man. Fuller defines true wealth as "our ability to deal successfully with our forward energetic regeneration and to provide increased degrees of freedom of initiation and non-interfering actions."[5]

Wealth as metaphysical know-how

He breaks it down into two parts, physical energy and metaphysical know-how, observing that we cannot run out of either one. Einstein's formula, $E=MC^2$ proves that energy as matter and energy as radiation are interchangeable variants, and building upon this "know-how," physicists have determined that physical energy is conserved, cannot be exhausted: "Energy is "finite and infinitely conserved."[6] Wealth as metaphysical know-how can only increase. We cannot learn less. Every time we make an experiment, we can only learn more. Every time we solve a problem, our wealth increases. Wealth by this standard is our mental, physical, spiritual ability to cope with the present and to plan and mold the future. The more we use it, the wealthier we are.

True wealth: The Edge

When I teach "True wealth," I show the film *The Edge* with Anthony Hopkins and Alec Baldwin.[7] This is a film that was relatively stillborn, and I wouldn't have seen it had it not been for a student who came in and said, "This film is exactly what you teach." *The Edge* features a billionaire, played by Anthony Hopkins. He is married to an incredibly beautiful model, who is having an affair with Alec Baldwin, a photographer. Hopkins has accompanied his wife, the photographer, and the camera crew on a photo shoot. As the movie begins, they have landed in Hopkins' personal jet, and are departing by helicopter over snow-capped peaks and icy-gray water to a remote lodge.

Lost in the Wilds

Hopkins, who has an encyclopedic memory, has been reading a book, *Lost in the Wilds*, a birthday gift given to him by his secretary before he left on the trip. Although Hopkins considers this gift a curious choice, it becomes quickly apparent that Baldwin and Hopkins' wife are having an affair; and one comes to suspect from the start that Baldwin, and perhaps Baldwin and the wife together, have a plot to kill the billionaire husband on this trip. The secretary may have anticipated this. As they board the helicopter, Hopkins' assistant tells him the weather should be agreeable and they should have no problems so long as they avoid flying at a height where they might encounter migrating geese. They plan to be gone just overnight, returning the next evening.

The rabbit and the panther

The book, the birthday gift, is just one of several highly symbolic items introduced at the opening of the film. Baldwin gives Hopkins a knife, and the lodge keeper says Hopkins must give him a coin, lest the cord of friendship be cut. The wife gives Hopkins a watch, affectionately engraved, "To the only man I have ever loved." He is moved. Baldwin is also wearing a new watch. We learn later that Baldwin's watch, a gift from the same woman, bears an engraving thanking him for "all the nights." Hopkins, whose conversation is learned and clever, is an endless storehouse of knowledge, facts, and information. It flows from him spontaneously. The lodge keeper, thinking he can trip him up, offers Hopkins $5 to tell him what is on the back of a wooden paddle with a panther on the front. Hopkins says, "It's a rabbit smoking a pipe." The lodge keeper turns over the paddle, and behold, Hopkins is right. The lodge keeper asks why the rabbit is smoking a pipe, and Hopkins replies, "Because the rabbit is smarter than the panther." The rabbit can afford to stop for a rest while the panther pursues. Baldwin is the panther; Hopkins is the rabbit.

The migrating geese

Circumstances cause Baldwin to go in search of a local trapper for a photo shoot. Hopkins, goaded on by his wife, accompanies him and one of his crew. They find a note on the trapper's cabin door that he is hunting at a spot about twenty miles north of his cabin, and they proceed by helicopter to that site. During the helicopter ride, with his ironic humor, Baldwin picks at Hopkins about the isolation, aloofness, separation of a rich man who can never know whether people really like him or whether they want something from him. Hopkins always replies, "Never feel sorry for a man who owns a plane." He asks Baldwin what he wants from him. Baldwin says he likes his wife. Just as Hopkins asks, "How are you planning to kill me?" the helicopter, flying low, collides with a flock of migrating geese. The geese break through the windshield, the helicopter goes down, and Hopkins, Baldwin, and Baldwin's assistant are the only survivors. They are lost in the frigid wild. Because Baldwin brought with him the note on the trapper's door, no one knows their destination.

Never feel sorry for a man who owns a plane

This man who owns a plane is by far the strongest of the three, not only in brainpower, but also in perseverance and courage. Hopkins emerges as the master mind, the problem solver, the center of their survival. He has with him literally only the clothes on his back, the knife Baldwin has just given him as a birthday present, the knowledge lodged in his brain, and an indomitable spirit. The survival book, which Hopkins was reading in the helicopter, is lost when they sink. The plot of the story pits man against man, man against himself, and man against bear, a Kodiak bear, about which they were warned by the lodge keeper, "Once this bear has tasted human flesh, it craves it."

The Kodiak bear

Hopkins draws upon every bit of knowledge he has. To set a course toward the south, he makes a magnet from a needle. A Kodiak bear finds them and begins to pursue them. They escape by toppling a log over the top of a waterfall. Hopkins is the last one over the log, precariously keeping his balance as the bear aggressively jumps up and down on the end. Hopkins falls into the river; and the other two scramble and stretch to save him from going over the waterfall. Baldwin tells Hopkins he was saved because they couldn't afford to lose him, articulating a synergy that leaves Hopkins strangely moved. Baldwin jests that Hopkins probably never had a friend. Hopkins reminds him, "Never feel sorry for a man who owns a plane."

Shame

When they discover this arduous adventure only leads them back to where they began, a walk in a circle, Baldwin and the assistant become hysterical. Hopkins admonishes them, "Why do men die in the woods. They die of shame." Hopkins acknowledges that his magnet didn't work because of his metal belt buckle. While he re-thinks their course, he attempts to distract the assistant from his fear by asking him to carve a spear from a stick with his knife. The assistant injures himself, a deep wound, and his blood draws the bear who attacks and devours him, leaving now only Hopkins and Baldwin and the bear who has tasted human flesh. When the stalking, flesh-craving bear becomes too much of a threat, Hopkins decides they must be the aggressor; they must kill the bear. He incites Baldwin to action by yelling, "Kill the Bear!" and the cry, "What one man can do, another can do." Hopkins lures the bear to fall on a spear, his weight becoming the force that kills him, a skillful implementation of leverage.

For all the nights: the dead fall

When Hopkins and Baldwin finally reach an abandoned cabin, it is near a river and houses a canoe. Baldwin, who can now see his way out on his own, is ready to carry out his original intent, to kill Hopkins. Hopkins, taking the warranty out of the watch box as paper to start a fire, finds the engravings ordered for the two watches by his wife. For the third time in the film, he asks to see Baldwin's watch. For the third time, Baldwin tells him the watch is broken. When Hopkins quotes the engraving, "for all the nights," Baldwin knows that Hopkins knows. He points the gun he found in the cabin at Hopkins; but Hopkins, unafraid, knowing Baldwin is a coward at heart, lures him, as he earlier lured the bear, to step on a bear trap, a dead fall. Baldwin falls into the hole and is impaled on the waiting spear. Even though Hopkins makes every effort to treat his wound and to take him out by canoe, Baldwin dies just as the search helicopter catches sight of them on the ground and comes in to rescue. He does a last good deed, saying "It's never too late for a kind gesture," by telling Hopkins his wife knew nothing of the murder plan.

Something unequivocal

Hopkins is the only survivor. He, too, makes a "kind gesture" by telling the press that the two dead men died saving his life. He, the rabbit, outsmarts both the bear and the panther. Hopkins' survival demonstrates his true wealth in action, the problem solving ability that empowered him not only to deal with his present circumstances but also to plan and forge ahead for his future, his regenerative power. He tells Baldwin, "All my life I wanted to do something unequivocal." The man who comes out of the wild is a far richer man than the one who went into the wild, for his wealth was tested and found adequate. He proved his capacity to cope with the present and to move purposefully and energetically toward the forward days of his life. His know-how expanded. We cannot learn less.

Symbolic and emblematic

Four statements from this film become symbolic, emblematic:

1) Never feel sorry for a man who owns a plane.

2) Why do men die in the woods? They die of shame.

3) Kill the bear!

4) What one man can do, another can do!

Not the root of all evil

When Hopkins comments, "Never feel sorry for a man who owns a plane," he is expressing a counter to the race consciousness—climate of opinion idea we carry around that if one is rich monetarily, one must be miserable. The statement "money is the root of all evil" is used to justify not having any; when in fact, the statement rendered correctly is "*love of money is the root of all evil*," covetousness. Actually, the free flow of funds, prosperity, a constant circulation of money in and out of a household, whether symbolized by a roll of bills in the pocket or a wad of bills on a money clip, eliminates at least half of the reason a marriage and family fall apart, financial stress: making ends meets, spouses accusing each other of not bringing in enough, spouses too strung out from struggle to have time or energy to be intimate with each other, fathers running away when they can't take it, turning to alcohol or drugs.

The master bedroom closet of the home tells the story to the realtor. If only the clothes of one partner are left, the other is gone. One finds a half-empty closet more frequently in homes ranging from $250,000 to $1,000,000. In this range people often overextend themselves, hoping, believing, or willing that their income will catch up to their expenses. When the price goes over a million dollars, the money usually isn't an issue. It is a story created and perpetuated by the media that the rich are more miserable than the rest of us.

Fear of not being enough

Hopkins observes, "Why do men die in the woods? They die of shame." This takes us back to "no mistakes." Survival in the woods tests physical endurance and mental alacrity, steadfastness of purpose and cunning. One feels completely exposed, naked. As Emily Dickinson says, "somebody" is "naked like a frog." Shame comes from fear of not being "enough" and doing it in public, whether observed by a human being, a bear, or a squirrel. When King Lear in Shakespeare's play makes a rash decision to accept his evil daughters' flattery and to abandon his faithful one, Cordelia, he also banishes his faithful servant, Kent. Kent, foreseeing Lear's mistreatment, that Lear's daughters will strip him of his power, asks to serve him. It is Kent's faithfulness that sustains Lear when he is naked in the storm, exposed to the elements, gone mad because of the betrayal of his daughters and the loss

of his retinue of soldiers, reduced from grandeur to homeless-
ness. This is the exchange between Lear and Kent, in disguise:
Lear says to him:
What wouldst thou?"
"Service."
"Who wouldst thou serve?"
    "You.
"Dost thou know me, fellow?"
"No, sire; but you have that in your countenance which I
would fain call 'master.'"
"What's that?"
"Authority.
King Lear, Act I, sc. iv, ll.24-31

Men die of shame in the woods because they have lost
touch with their inner "authority," with their identity, with
their center. Peter Goldberg, a psychoanalytic historian,
researched the reasons why the victims of the holocaust,
learned, capable, intelligent professional human beings,
allowed themselves to be herded and slaughtered like cattle.
He concluded that when their clothes were removed, when
they were naked, they no longer had the outer reinforcing
symbolic garments to remind them of their identity as effective human beings. They lost their "authority"; they died of
shame. "Why do men die in the woods? They die of shame."

The cry of the hunter: Kill the Bear!

To "Kill the Bear!" Hopkins and Baldwin need to call upon
every atom of adrenalin their bodies can produce. This cry,
"Kill the Bear!" organizes the human body and spirit in purpose, in cause, in determination, in defiance against weakness

and vulnerability. At this moment, every other concern in life falls away. There is only one intent. It is a commitment that one makes to life, to continue living, and the human body and spirit rise to the occasion. When Hopkins accompanies "Kill the Bear!" with "What one man can do, another can do!" he is bringing Baldwin, the weaker of the two, along with him. These words penetrate his mind and spirit, and his inner resources marshal to the occasion.

To the edge of possibility

We do not know who we are until we are tested. This is true leadership. When Emerson describes Napoleon leading his men up, into, and across the mountains, he did it with the battle cry, "There shall be no Alps." And there were no Alps. The Alps were conquered. "Napoleon," says Emerson, "went to the edge of his possibility."[8] The same thing happens to Baldwin as he is challenged by Hopkins: "What one man can do another can do!" Hopkins and Baldwin act with a most remarkable synergy to perform a super-human feat. Battle cries have been used throughout the ages by primitive tribes preparing for the hunt, by soldiers preparing to meet the enemy: "What one man can do, another can do!" "Kill the Bear!" Hopkins all his life has wanted to do "something unequivocal." When he goes to the "edge of his possibility," when he kills the bear, it is done.

The Store of Knowledge

The metaphysical know-how demonstrated by Hopkins in the film cannot be purchased, and it "grows like Topsy." Every time we use it, we have more, because we cannot learn less. Yet, to go back to the story of the loaves and the fishes, back to the true metaphysical message of leverage, we find the "metaphysical know-how" kind of wealth now has a traditional monetary value. When Microsoft Corporation surpassed the $500 billion mark, it brought inextricably into marriage "true wealth" and traditionally measured wealth. When I say "traditionally measured," I refer to the measure of wealth in gold, in currency, in jewels, in stocks, in bonds, in real estate equities.

Financial equivalent

This significant advancement in placing a financial equivalent upon a "store of knowledge, upon "intellectual property," occurred almost simultaneously with the announcement that Great Britain has begun selling off large deposits of gold. The gold standard, which Maynard Keynes considered barbarism, is being globally devalued in importance, may one day be even discarded. England no longer feels that it needs to keep gold as backing to its currency. Other nations concur. The sell-off of gold lowers its value on the world market.

Symbolic mediators

Concurrently, the selling of knowledge, computer software, grows. As its price goes down, volume goes up, expanding the availability to a broader base of consumers. When asked in an interview by Barbara Walters about the value of Microsoft's stock, Bill Gates said he never wakes up in the morning thinking about it. All he thinks about is creating better software, a knowledge enabler, a facilitator, or as Bill Gates calls it, a "mediator." He says, "Information tools are symbolic mediators. They amplify intellect rather than muscle· [9]

Moore's Law

When man combines the tool with true wealth, i.e. the stored data with the know-how to use it, it's almost impossible to imagine where this will take him. In 1965 Gordon Moore predicted the capacity of a computer chip would double every year. When that proved out, in 1975 he predicted the chip capacity would double every two years. In 1995 it was doubling every eighteen months. This average rate of increase, doubling every eighteen months, is now called "Moore's Law." That means our access to data or to information is doubling at that speed.

Exponential Function

This doubling of numbers is the "exponential function." It is illustrated in the fable of the Indian king who asked the man who invented the game of chess what reward he would like. The inventor used the sixty-four chessboard squares as a basis for his request. He asked that one grain of wheat be placed on the first square, and that on each successive square, the amount be doubled that of the previous one. By square eight he had 255; by square sixteen 65,535; by square twenty-four 8.4 million.[10] Think about doing this with a single penny. The popular program "Who Wants to be a Millionaire?" effectively uses the exponential function. In just sixteen questions, the contestants who last are up to $1,000,000 by doubling the wager on each question.

True Wealth in action
Our wealthy new immigrants: the Vietnamese

The unlimited growth and application of knowledge, of know-how, is true wealth in action. It walks around with us, in us, available to us at every living moment. The more we use it, the more we have. When we say that the United States is the wealthiest nation in the world, our attention is usually to the financial and the monetary; yet our real wealth is a drowsy giant, waiting for us to pay attention to it, to mobilize it. As I look across the people of America today, I feel privileged to be able to teach, to lead, to interact with and to support one of the truly wealthiest segments of our society, the Vietnamese immigrants.

Re-education Camps

The twenty-fifth anniversary of the 1975 fall of Saigon healed some of the wounds of the Viet Nam War and focused attention on the Vietnamese immigrants and their activity, their productivity, in their adopted new home, the USA. Many Americans do not realize that the Vietnamese who came here after the fall of Saigon in 1975 were granted special immigration opportunities because they had been vigorously engaged in our American effort in the Viet Nam War and had worked intimately with our personnel. In their past lives many of these immigrants were business-men, doctors, pharmacists, generals, mayors, leaders, professional people with high degrees and training. When the North Vietnamese Communists took over, the homes and possessions of the men and their families were seized, the men were placed in "Re-education Camps," concentration camps, and the women and the children were left to fend for themselves, without resources.

Women in new roles

The women, for the most part, had been in traditional family roles, with husbands to provide for them and the family. They found themselves now head of the households, forced to work, to scratch to earn a living for the first time, with everything against them because they were rejected, outside the Communist establishment. These women, especially, discovered within themselves resilience and an ability to meet challenges for growth that would have remained undiscovered. An ability to do needlework turned them into seamstresses; an ability to cook turned them into vendors of their best dishes at the market; an ability to argue and bargain turned them into merchants, buying and selling, trading to keep alive. The wives not only had to take care of the family left at home, but also they needed to visit their husbands in the Re-Education Camps to augment the meager rations provided by the Communists. Often this required a long trip, ten to twelve hours in a single day, or sometimes several days, of travel. The women worked collectively to support one another.

Emigration: the big picture

My students write with thanksgiving and praise of the efforts of their wives, their mothers, their sisters, their grandmothers, their aunts, to care for the family and to enable them to prepare for the most important move of their life, the emigration to the United States. Because the life of the individual is not singular, not just I, but "I" as "I" interact with others, the "big picture" effectively realized is a collective adoption of an idea. When the men returned home, there was nothing of their former life to be recaptured. They collectively conceived of a "big picture" of coming to the United States to create a new life for themselves. They were able to mobilize the three big D's: devotion, dedication, and discipline. To pay for the travel, they sold whatever material wealth they still possessed: gold, jewels, art. The Vietnamese have stories of the harrowing voyages that they undertook, attacked by pirates, robbed, raped, and pillaged.

Survival of boat hardships

One of my students, a woman who has now been here for eighteen years, still cannot speak of her departure without crying. Her mother stayed behind to make it possible for her to go. There were ninety people on the boat. A storm moved in; and when the storm was over, there were only forty-five. This woman, who came here penniless and unable to speak English, now is married, has two daughters, owns a home, has brought her mother to the United States, and has just been accepted in the nursing program at California State University at Long Beach.

Holding camps

Those who were successful in their voyages found themselves in holding camps in Malaysia, in Singapore, in the Philippines, waiting until a sponsor would assist them to come here to the United States. When they finally arrived here, they were without funds, without the language, without a job, often without even a relative to care for them. They didn't know how to drive a car, even how to operate the household appliances we all take for granted. Yet, they went to work. They got jobs at minimum wage. They went to school at night to learn English as a second language. They worked together. I have so many inspiring stories of persistence and vision from among my students. I will share two of them with you, representing two generations. Since these stories have been told by many who experienced similar trials and success, I have not included the names; for I wish to honor all of these people for their strength and resilience.

A former general

One of my students was a general in the Vietnamese Army. He had owned his own successful business before joining the army; and he owned a home, with a wife and three daughters. After the fall of Saigon in 1975, he spent eight years in the Re-Education camp. Soon after he got out, his wife, who had cared for his daughters during his incarceration, died. He made arrangements to escape by boat, bringing his daughters with him. They spent fifteen months in the Philippines waiting for a sponsor. When he finally got to the U.S., he took a job on an assembly line at minimum wage to support his family, taking first a room in someone's home, then renting a one-bedroom apartment. His daughters began attending school, struggling with the language.

The whole family enrolled in ESL classes, English as a Second Language. Because he was so efficient at what he did, he had a series of promotions at the company where he worked. He supported his daughters through high school and then through college. With scholarships to reward their diligent study, they have all graduated from four-year colleges and universities, one of them from UC Berkeley. In the summer of 1998, the third daughter was married, and he brought me pictures of the wedding. This gentleman has not remarried and has sacrificed everything to his daughters' success. In his earnest desire to improve his writing skill in my class, he did at least six rough drafts for every paper that he wrote.

Four escape attempts

Another of my students, the son of a Vietnamese officer, was an honor student in his high school when the war ended and his father was sent to a Re-education camp. Because of his father's "crime," he was not allowed to enter a university, even though he had high scores to qualify him. He made his first escape with a group of 65 on a boat. A typhoon pushed them back to Viet Nam. He was captured, spent two years in prison, and released to try again. It was only after his fourth attempt at escape that he made it to Galang Island in Thailand.

When he finally, after several months, had an interview with U.S. Immigration, he was told he was not accepted because he didn't have a sponsor. An American priest at the camp, impressed by the young man's persistence and self-discipline, interceded on his behalf and convinced his older brother in California to sponsor him. One month after the young man arrived from Thailand, his sponsor died from a heart attack, and he found himself alone again. He took two jobs, one picking strawberries during the day, another washing dishes in a restaurant at night. He rented a room in a private home, and he sent money back to his family in Viet Nam from his meager earnings. Within the next six years, he was able to have the rest of his family sponsored to come here, now lives with them together in a single house as he did in Viet Nam, has completed his A.A. degree at a community college, and is attending Long Beach State to get a B.A. degree in graphic design.

Little Saigon

In the area of Orange County in California, designated Little Saigon, you can chart by street the movement of this hard-working, self-disciplined, intelligent, persevering group of immigrants. As their neighborhood expands, they improve the environment. The streets are neat and tidy; their shops, stores, and professional offices have clean windows; their homes and apartment buildings are in good repair with flowers planted in the yards. Purposeful activity directs their movement. Education is held in the highest place in this community, only second to the family. If we wonder why UCLA is an anagram for "United Caucasians Lost among Asians," and why the University of California at Irvine is dominated by Asians, it is because the Asian immigrants have a" big picture" with definite goals, work hard, never quit, and tirelessly seek to use and develop every bit of God-given *true wealth* that they have.

Lofty aspirations

Their aspirations, their big pictures are lofty. They want to be medical doctors, dentists, pharmacists, engineers, computer network specialists, computer programmers, accountants, financial analysts, teachers, nurses. They are making a great contribution to our culture by sharing the intensity of their commitment to excellence. A friend who has been a patient at the VA Hospital speaks of the improved care since Vietnamese medical residents are on the staff.

Elementary school teachers who have Vietnamese students tell me that they are their best students. It was exemplified for me one day when I was having my nails done at, yes, a Vietnamese nail salon. The daughter of the owner, seven years old, answers the phone, makes the change, and places the orders for her mother. Very pleased with herself and extremely self-confident, she told me that she knew three languages: Vietnamese, English, and Mexican. I said, "Well, 'Mexican' is actually 'Spanish.'" "Oh," she said, elated, "Then I know four languages: Vietnamese, English, Mexican, and Spanish."

Risk-taking visionaries: our national wealth

Most of us came at one time from the same risk-taking, visionary, persevering, self-disciplined stock as this most recent immigrant group. This is the "true wealth" of the American Society. We have been able to convert the capital wealth of this country to greater productivity and expansion by the constant increase of our metaphysical know-how. When we regard wealth in this way, there can only be expansion, exponential expansion. This means there can only be increased abundance, that there is enough. Fuller cites the official U.S. Census of 1810 that valued the national wealth of the United States at three billion dollars. He observes at that time we had no telegraph, no electro-magnetics, no mass-produced steel, no railroads, no wireless, no X-ray, no electric light, no power by wire, no electric motor, no knowledge of atoms or electrons.[11] All of these discoveries and a myriad more have been made through the exercise of our true wealth, our metaphysical know how.

Even wealth from war

Even when man is at his worst, in waging war, our true wealth, metaphysical know-how is at work. In World War II, suddenly we had money for the war effort when before there wasn't enough money. We were still in a Great Depression state of mind. How did we do this? Through leverage! We sold bonds; we printed paper currency. We gave the paper currency to manufacturers who put people to work and paid them with paper currency, and then they bought things with it.

Greater production capability

Fuller points out that at the end of World War I, Germany, England, France, Belgium, Italy, Japan, Russia, and especially the United States had "greater production capabilities than those with which they had entered."[12] By the end of World War II, the effects were even more empowering: 1) A more effective complex of industrial tools was created and developed; 2) Obsolete "tool-enclosing brick and wood structures" were destroyed and had to be replaced with modern facilities; 3) We had the benefit of the "synergetic surprise of alternative or 'substitute' technologies"; 4) Metals were destroyed and reinvested in new, higher-performance tools.[13]

Metaphysical and monetary wealth: interconnected

The United States, goaded about the deficit with charts from Perot, worried and fussing about the deficit during the Reagan/Bush terms of office, is presently predicting a thirteen trillion dollar surplus in ten years. Notice how integrally connected is metaphysical wealth and monetary wealth. Our stock market is booming in great part because of intellectual property investments: software, Internet, communication. There is no limit to where we can go. Nothing truly exists except the mind in action as thought. As we take control of our thinking and tap into our true wealth, our wealth multiplies exponentially. I offer the following exercise as your personal wealth inventory. Use it not only to impress yourself with the enormous wealth you possess, but also to assure you that there is always enough, indeed, more than enough.

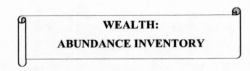

WEALTH:

ABUNDANCE INVENTORY

Fuller tells us that *"wealth is the product of the progressive mastery of matter by mind"* and that *"know-how can only increase."* In the light of this definition, I know I am wealthy because I have tapped into my know-how by solving the following problems.

At home:

_____

_____

_____

_____

_____

_____

At work:

_____

_____

_____

_____

_____

In my personal life:

_____

_____

_____

_____

_____

_____

How does this statement by Fuller corroborate your experience: *"...Every time man makes a new experiment he always learns more. He cannot learn less. He may learn that what he thought was true was not true."* Can you think of three instances when you have "learned more?"

1.
_____
2.
_____
3.
_____

I have always considered wealth material possessions because:

My parents believed:

_____

_____

_____

_____

In my community the wealthiest and most influential people were:

_____

_____

_____

_____

When I go to the movies and watch television, wealthy people are portrayed as:

_____

_____

_____

My teachers encouraged me to:

_____

_____

_____

_____

The thoughts I had today that expressed "Scarcity" or "Fear" that I don't have enough are:

_____

_____

_____

_____

The thoughts I had today that expressed a feeling of abundance are:

_____

_____

_____

_____

_____

_____

All it would take to know I have *enough* would be:

_____

_____

_____

_____

_____

_____

I can use my true wealth, my "know-how," along with my understanding of leverage, to create abundance in my life by:

_____

_____

_____

_____

_____

_____

Conclusion

Pragmatic idealism

Pragmatic idealism might be the most apt description for Fuller's *Operating Manual for Spaceship Earth*. When he wrote this little book in 1969, he compared humanity to a tiny chick just at the point where its ready to break through the shell, when the nutriment is almost gone and the chick is ready to move with its own legs and wings:

> My own picture of humanity today finds us just about to step out from amongst the pieces of our just one-second-ago broken eggshell. Our innocent, trial-and-error-sustaining nutriment is exhausted. We are faced with an entirely new relationship to the universe. We are going to have to spread our wings of intellect and fly or perish; that is, we must dare immediately to fly by the generalized principles governing universe and not by the ground rules of yesterday's superstitious and erroneously conditioned reflexes. And as we attempt competent thinking, we immediately begin to reemploy our innate drive for comprehensive understanding.[1]

Free: thoughts, ideas, promises

Certainly we have broken through that shell, and we have begun to fly by the generalized principles of leverage, synergy, and true wealth at exponential rates. The distribution is still uneven. We have those who "got it" and those who still are "getting it." The obstacles, however, that used to hold us back

283

aren't there anymore. We all have access to the same tools that Bill Gates has. Great Pirates can't set limits, can't control the flow of knowledge. True wealth is abundant, growing exponentially, and free. Thoughts are free, ideas are free, promises are free. We can all use *Expectation, Belief,* and *Word,* all free, at any second of any minute of any hour to create exactly what we want. The personal employment of competent thinking and comprehensive understanding will expand for each of us as we enlarge our personal big picture. Prosperity must follow as the night follows the day.

Perfect mind, perfect plan, perfect beneficence

The idea of a perfect mind, a perfect plan, a perfect beneficence becomes more evident the more we discover about how things work. Each element of the operation of the Universe that we figure out, working backward to create an operating manual, leaves us more in awe of the mind of the Maker. It makes believers out of scientists who may have begun with an honest doubt, as the poet Matthew Arnold observes, "There lives more faith in honest doubt/ Believe me than in half the creeds." The physicist, Erwin Schrodinger, comes to this realization when he describes man's union with this perfect mind in his book, *My View of the World*: "All of us living beings belong together in as much as we are all in reality sides or aspects of one single being, which may perhaps in western terminology be called God while in the Upanishads its name is Brahman."[2]

Walt Whitman speaks of this in *Leaves of Grass*:
I have said that the soul is not more than the body,
And I have said that the body is not more than the soul,
And nothing, not God is greater to one than one's self is,
And whoever walks a furlong without sympathy walks

to his own funeral, dressed in his shroud,
And I or you pocketless of a dime may purchase the
    pick of the earth,
And to glance with an eye or show a bean in its pod confounds
    the learning of all times,
And there is no trade or employment but the young
    man following it may become a hero,
And there is no object so soft but it makes a hub for
    the wheeled universe,
And any man or woman shall stand cool and supercilious
    before a million universes.
And I call to mankind, Be not curious about God,
For I who am curious about each am not curious about God,
No array of terms can say how much I am at peace about
    God and about death.
I hear and behold God in every object, yet I understand God
    not in the least,
Nor do I understand who there can be more wonderful than
    myself.

Why should I wish to see God better than this day?
I see something of God each hour of the twenty-four,
    and each moment then,
In the faces of men and women I see God, in my own face in
    the glass;
I find letters from God dropped in the street, and every one
    is signed by God's name,
And I leave them where they are, for I know that
    others will punctually come forever and forever.
Walt Whitman 1855 ll. 1262-1280

Be fooled out of your limits

Awe of God increases our awe of us. We are the only creature who can be whatever we choose to be, can select our

incarnation. We can think it, and we can be it, like Emerson's young man from New Hampshire, a cat landing on its feet, tiller of the earth, poet, statesman, astronaut, frogman, painter, sculptor. Man has "visions that fool him out of his limits," the poet Robinson Jeffers declares: "Humanity is the mold to break away from, the crust to break through, the coal to break into fire, the atom to be split."[3]

Be fooled out of your limits. Catch fire. Be as Shelley's poet, ignited by truth.

Know that you are man, you are woman, you are one with the mind that created this universe. Accept the gift.

> To the glory of Him that moves all things,
> penetrates through the universe and is resplendent
> in one part more, and in another less.
>   Dante, Paradiso, ll. 1-3

Reference Notes

Introduction

1. Ralph Waldo Emerson, *Selected Writings of Emerson*, ed. Donald McQuade (NewYork: The Modern Library, 1981), p. xvii. All references to Emerson are from this edition and the notes hereafter will indicate them by *Emerson* and the page number. You may find these quotations in any edition of Emerson's essays.

2. R. Buckminster Fuller, *Operating Manual for Spaceship Earth* (New York: E. P. Dutton, 1963). All references are from this edition and the notes hereafter will indicate them by *Manual* and the page number.

3. *Emerson*, p. xxiv.

4. Ameron, Ltd, 800 Wickham Avenue, Mattituck, NY 11952 offers re-prints of Fuller's *Operating Manual for Spaceship Earth*.

5. Ernest Holmes, *The Science of Mind* (New York: G.P. Putnam's Sons, 1988), p.xxvi.

Part 1. Life's Sentence

The Sentence

1. *Emerson*, p.2.

2. Franz Kafka, "The Judgment," *Psychological Fiction*, ed. Morris Beja (Glenview, Illinois: Scott, Foresman & Company, 1971).

3. Franz Kafka, "The Metamorphosis," *Classics of Modern Fiction: Ten Short Novels*, ed. Irving Howe (New York: Harcourt Brace Jovanovich, Inc., 1980).

Making Ends Meet

1. *Emerson*, p. 15.

2. *Manual*, p. 16.

3. David Friedman, "The Fate of a Nation," *LA Times*, Sunday, August 20, 1995, "Opinion," 1.

4. Marla Dickinson, "The Six O'Clock Scramble," *LA Times*, August 1, 1999, A3.

5. Mary McNamara, "Our Culture of Efficiency Has Made Life Harder," *LA Times*, September 6, 1999, E1.

6. Dirk Johnson "America Has Become a Nation of Nibblers," *Orange County Register*, August 1, 1999, News 1.

7. Robert Kiyosaki, with Sharon L. Lechter, *Rich Dad Poor Dad* (Paradise Valley, Arizona: TechPress, Inc., 1998.

Inherent Evil

1. *Emerson*, p. 29.

2. *Emerson*, p. 29.

3. Nathaniel Hawthorne, *Tales and Sketches* (New York: The Viking Press, 1972), p. 17.

4. Ibid., p. 31.

5. Ibid., p. 32.

6. Ibid., p. 32.

Limits: Living Someone Else's Dream

1. *Emerson*, p. 43.

2. James Joyce, "Araby," *Dubliners* (New York: The Viking Press, 1958) p. 44. All quotations from this text.

Too Easy: The Oxen and the Eagle

1. *Emerson*, p. 58.

2. Robert Frost, "Fire and Ice," *The Poems of Robert Frost* (New York: The Modern Library, 1930), p. 64.

Part 2: A Conceptual Framework

We are all Astronauts

1. Miguel de Cervantes Saavedra, *Don Quixote*, trans. Samuel Putnam (New York: The Viking Press, 1949), p. 74.

2. *Manual*, p. 75.

3. Carl Sagan, *Cosmos* (New York: Random House, 1980), p. 80.

Trial and Error

1. Emily Dickinson, "'Tis So Much Joy," *Selected Poems of Emily Dickinson* (New York: Random House, 1924), p.82.

2. Emerson, p. 82.

3. Sagan, p. 84.

4. Ibid., p. 85.

5. Ibid., p. 85.

6. Ibid., p. 85

7. Ibid., p. 85.

8. Ibid., p. 87.

9. Ibid., p. 87.

The Metaphysical Context

1. *Emerson*, p. 90.

2. G. Montgomery, "The Mind in Motion," *Discover*, March 1989. p.93.

3. David Perkins, ed., *English Romantic Writers* (New York: Harcourt, Brace, & World, 1967, 1073.

4. Ibid., 1085.

5. Ibid.

6. *Emerson*, p. 102.

7. Perkins, p. 102.

8. Eric Lavigne, "Squaring the Circle: An esoteric perspective on the classic puzzle," *Parabola*, Summer, 2000, p. 103.

9. Christian Wertenbaker, "One and One Make One: The mystery of the outer world and the inner world," *Parabola*, Summer, 2000, p. 105.

Part 3. Tool Kit of Concepts

The Great Pirates

1. Nathaniel Hawthorne, *The House of the Seven Gables* (Cutchogue, New York: Buccaneer Books, 1987), p. 110.

2. Niccolo Machiavelli, *The Prince*, trans. T. G. Bergin (New York: Appleton-Century, Crofts, 1947), p. 110.

3. *Emerson*, p. 134.

Piano Tops

1. *Emerson*, p. 140.

2. *Manual*, p. 141.

3. *Emerson*, p. 153.

4. *Manual*, p. 153.

5. Napoleon Hill, *Think and Grow Rich* (New York: Fawcett Books, 1960), p. 154.

No Mistakes

1. Dante Alleghieri, *Dante's Inferno*, trans. Mark Musa (Bloomington: Indiana University Press, 1971), Canto I, l. 1-9.

2. *Emerson*, p. 163.

3. *Manual*, p. 168.

4. Sophocles, *Oedipus the King*, trans. David Grene, *An Anthology of Greek Drama*, ed. C.A. Robinson, Jr. (New York: Holt, Rinehart and Winston, 1960), p. 173.

5. Ibid., p. 173.

6. Rob Turner, "Investors' Biggest Mistakes," *Money Magazine*, September, 1999, p. 177.

7. Ibid., p. 81.

8. *Manual*, p. 180.

Leverage: More with Less

1. *Emerson*, p. 186

2. Maynard Keynes, "The General Theory of Employment," *Quarterly Journal of Economics*, Feb. 1937, reprinted in S. E. Harris, ed. *The New Economics*, p. 189. Reprinted in Axel Leijonhufvud, *On Keynesian Economics and the Economics of Keynes: A Study in Monetary Theory* (London: Oxford University Press, 1968), p. 163.

3. Ibid.

4. Manual, p. 191

5. Keynes, p. 46, reprinted in Leijonhufvud, p. 201.

Synergy

1. *Emerson*, p.211.

2. *Emerson*, p.211.

3. Herman Melville, "Bartelby the Scrivener A Story of Wall Street," *Psychological Fiction*, ed. Morris Beja (Glenville, Illinois: Scott, Foresman & Company, 1971, p.212.

4. The test with the DISC classification in the results is the Personal Profile System trademarked by Carlson Learning in Minneapolis, Minnesota.
To order the test or to get more information about it, call 800 777 9897.

5. Here are some web sites that offer various psychological tests to determine whether your career is right for you: keirsey.com, ansir.com, od-online.com, queendom.com, review.com/birkman/tms.com.au/questionnaire.html, com, universityoflife.com, test.com, ncsu.edu/unity/lockers/ users/ l/ikj/career_key.html

Big Picture

1. Joseph Campbell, *Myths to Live By* (New York: The Viking Press, 1972), p. 233.

2. *Emerson*, p. 233.

3. Virginia Woolf, *To the Lighthouse* (New York: Harcourt, Brace & World, Inc., 1927), p. 235.

4. Ibid., p. 235.

5. Ibid., p. 235.

6. Ibid., p. 236.

7. Ibid., p. 236.

8. Ibid., p. 237.

9. Ibid.

10. Ibid., p. 237.

11. *Manual*, p. 238.

12. Ibid., p. 238.

13. Ibid., p. 238.

True Wealth

1. George S. Clason, *The Richest Man in Babylon* (New York: Penguin Books, 1955), p. 257.

2. *Emerson*, p. 257.

3. Ibid., p. 257.

4. *Manual*, p. 258.

5. Ibid., p. 259.

6. Ibid., p. 259.

7. *The Edge*, Twentieth Century Fox, 1997, starring Anthony Hopkins and Alec Baldwin.

8. Emerson, p. 267.

9. Bill Gates, *The Road Ahead* (New York: Penguin Books, 1993), p. 268.

10. Ibid., p. 269.

11. *Manual*, p. 276.

12. Ibid., p 277.

13. Ibid., p. 277.

Conclusion

1. *Manual*, p. 283.

2. Erwin Schrodinger, *My View of the World*, (Cambridge: Cambridge University Press, 1964), p. 284.

3. Robinson Jeffers, *Roan Stallion, Tamar, and Other Poems* (New York: Horace Liveright, 1925), p. 286.

Bibliography

Robert Browning, *Poems of Robert Browning*, ed. Donald Smalley: A Riverside Edition (Boston: Houghton Mifflin Co., 1956).

Joseph Campbell, *Myths to Live By* (New York: The Viking Press, 1972).

Joseph Campbell, *The Power of Myth with Bill Moyers*, ed. Betty Sue Flowers (New York: Doubleday 1988).

Miguel de Cervantes Saavedra, *Don Quixote*, trans. Samuel Putnam (New York: The Viking Press, 1949).

George S. Clason, *The Richest Man in Babylon* (New York: Penguin Books, 1955)

Dante Alleghieri, *Dante's Inferno*, trans. Mark Musa (Bloomington: Indiana University Press, 1971).

Emily Dickinson, *Selected Poems of Emily Dickinson* (New York: Random House, 1924).

John Donne, *The Poems of John Donne*, ed. Herbert Grierson (London: Oxford University Press, 1949.

Ralph Waldo Emerson, *Selected Writings of Emerson*, ed. Donald McQuade (New York: The Modern Library, 1981).

Favorite Folktales from Around the World, ed. Jan Yolen (New York: Pantheon Books, 1986).

Robert Frost, *The Poems of Robert Frost* (New York: The Modern Library, 1930)

R. Buckminster Fuller, *Operating Manual for Spaceship Earth* (New York: E. P. Dutton, 1963).

Bill Gates, *The Road Ahead* (New York: Penguin Books, 1993)

Nathaniel Hawthorne, *The House of the Seven Gables* (Cutchogue, New York: Buccaneer Books, 1987).

Nathaniel Hawthorne, *Tales and Sketches* (New York: The Viking Press, 1972).

Napoleon Hill, *Think and Grow Rich* (New York: Fawcett Books, 1960).

Ernest Holmes, *The Science of Mind* (New York: G.P. Putnam's Sons, 1988).

Robinson Jeffers, *Roan Stallion, Tamar, and Other Poems* (New York: Horace Liveright, 1925), p. 232.

James Joyce, *Dubliners* (New York: The Viking Press, 1958).

Franz Kafka, "The Judgment," *Psychological Fiction*, ed. Morris Beja (Glenview, Illinois: Scott, Foresman & Company, 1971).

Franz Kafka, "The Metamorphosis," *Classics of Modern Fiction: Ten Short Novels*, ed. Irving Howe (New York: Harcourt Brace Jovanovich, Inc., 1980).

Robert Kiyosaki, with Sharon L. Lechter, *Rich Dad Poor Dad* (Paradise Valley, Arizona: TechPress, Inc., 1998).

Eric Lavigne, "Squaring the Circle: An esoteric perspective on the classic puzzle," *Parabola*, Summer 2000, pp. 34-41.

Axel Leijonhufvud, *On Keynesian Economics and the Economics of Keynes: A Study in Monetary Theory* (London: Oxford University Press, 1968).

Niccolo Machiavelli, *The Prince*, trans. T. G. Bergin (New York: Appleton-Century, Crofts, 1947).

Herman Melville, "Bartelby the Scrivener A Story of Wall Street," *Psychological Fiction*, ed. Morris Beja (Glenville, Illinois: Scott, Foresman & Company, 1971) p.235-265.

John Milton, The Portable Milton (New York: The Viking Press, 1949).

G. Montgomery, "The Mind in Motion," *Discover*, March 1989, pp. 58-68.

David Perkins, ed., *English Romantic Writers* (New York: Harcourt, Brace, & World, 1967).

Jeremy Rifkin, *The End of Work* (New York: G. B. Putnam's Sons, 1995)

Carl Sagan, *Cosmos* (New York: Random House, 1980).

Erwin Schrodinger, *My View of the World*, (Cambridge: Cambridge University Press, 1964).

William Shakespeare, *Shakespeare: The Complete Works*, ed. G.B. Harrison (New York: Harcounrt Brace and Company, 1948).

Sophocles, *Oedipus the King*, trans. David Grene, *An Anthology of Greek Drama*, ed. C.A. Robinson, Jr. (New York: Holt, Rinehart and Winston, 1960).

Lord Alfred Tennyson, *Tennyson's Poetry* (New York: W.W. Norton & Company, Inc., 1971).

Rob Turner, "Investors' Biggest Mistakes," *Money Magazine*, September, 1999, 77-88.

Christian Wertenbaker, "One and One Make One: The mystery of the outer world and the inner world," *Parabola*, Summer, 2000, 6-12.

Walt Whitman, *Leaves of Grass,* Version of the First (1855) Edition, section 48, lines 1262-1280, Ed. Malcolm Cowley (New York: The Viking Press, 1961).

Virginia Woolf, *To the Lighthouse,* (New York: Harcourt, Brace & World, Inc., 1927).

Index